COLLECTED POEMS

JOSEPHINE MILES

COLLECTED POEMS

1930–83

UNIVERSITY OF ILLINOIS PRESS

Urbana and Chicago

Publication of this work was supported in part by a grant from the Illinois Arts Council, a state agency.

Manufactured in the United States of America

This book is printed on acid-free paper.

Library of Congress Cataloging in Publication Data

Miles, Josephine, 1911–
Collected poems.

I. Title
PS3525.I4835A6 1983 811′.52 82-11014

ISBN 0-252-01017-5

Acknowledgment is made to publishers of earlier books from which some of these poems were selected: *Trial Balances*, Macmillan, 1935; *Lines at Intersection*, Macmillan, 1939; *Poems on Several Occasions*, New Directions, 1941; *Local Measures*, Reynal and Hitchcock, 1946; *Prefabrications*, Indiana University Press, 1955; *Poems 1930–1960*, Indiana University Press, 1960; *Civil Poems*, Oyez, 1966; *Kinds of Affection*, Wesleyan University Press, 1967; *Fields of Learning*, Oyez, 1968; *To All Appearances*, University of Illinois Press, 1974; *Coming to Terms*, University of Illinois Press, 1979.

Acknowledgment is also made to those publications in which some of these poems first appeared: Poems from *Trial Balances:* in *College Verse, The New Republic, Poetry: A Magazine of Verse, Saturday Review of Literature;* from *Lines at Intersection: The Forum, The Nation, The New Republic, Poetry, Saturday Review of Literature, Scribner's Magazine;* from *Poems on Several Occasions: Accent, Common Sense, Kenyon Review, The New Republic, Poetry, Southern Review;* from *Local Measures: Accent, Circle, Kenyon Review, New Directions 1941, Pacific, Poetry: A Magazine of Verse, Rocky Mountain Review, Sewanee Review, Southern Review;* from *Prefabrications: Beloit Poetry Journal, Contemporary Poetry, Experiment, Furioso, Hudson Review, Kenyon Review, Occident, Pacific Spectator, Perspective, Poetry: A Magazine of Verse, Recurrence, Sewanee Review, Voices, Western Review, Yale Review;* from *Poems 1930–1960: Beloit Poetry Journal, Experiment, Evergreen Review, Furioso, Hudson Review, Harper's Bazaar, Kenyon Review, Listen* (England), *The New Yorker, Poetry: A Magazine of Verse, Poetry Northwest, Perspective, Prairie Schooner, Recurrence, Sewanee Review, Voices, Western Review, Yale Review;* from *Fields of Learning: Hudson Review;* from *To All Appearances: American Poems, Cafe Solo, Goat's Head, Hyperion, The Nation, New Mexico, The New Yorker, Poetry Now, Southern Review, Street Poems, Voyages;* from *Coming To Terms: Ascent, Beloit Poetry Journal, California Quarterly, Gramercy Review, Hawaii Review, Hyperion, Mill Mountain Review, New England Review, The New Yorker, Plainsong, Poetry Now, San Jose Quarterly, University of California, San Diego, Woman Poet, Yankee.*

And acknowledgment is made to the publications in which the following uncollected poems first appeared.

"Vigils," "Faces," and "Sleep" are reprinted with permission from *Poetry*, 139 (Oct., 1981); "Afternoon Walk" first appeared in *Conjunctions*, 1 (Winter, 1981-82) and also appeared in *Iowa Review*, 12 (Spring-Summer, 1981); "Ions" is reprinted with the permission of *Women Writing Poetry in America* (Stanford University) and the Matrix Press; "West from Ithaca," "He Said" (retitled "Promise"), "Capitol," and "For Magistrates" appeared in *Epoch*, 31 (Fall-Winter, 1982); "World" in *Poetry East*, 9/10 (Spring, 1983).

Acknowledgment is also made with much appreciation to Deborah Willis for steadfast aid.

CONTENTS

Trial Balances
and Other Early Poems (1930s)

from

Trial Balances and Other Early Poems

1930s

MORNING IN BRANCHES

Year upon year of sunlight lying here,
Decades of gold upon a length of bark;
Archaic speech of leaves that spin their shadows
To fitful flecks of dark:

This time will end with death of shade at noon
As crescent light began it, long ago.
This branch and I will be a morning older—
Year upon year of sunlight older than you know.

SPEED LIMIT

There is a heap of sky out tonight, brother,
There is a heap of air round and about.
Speed on this road, turn off on another,
And we'll go out.

Out into the wide sky,
Suddenly.

Keep two wheels down on the street here, brother,
Curves have a way of riding on wind tonight.
Hill on one side, air on every other,
We'll stick tight.

Tight to the small ground moving steadily
In so much sky!

NAME

Father, father, says the sea's edge,
Crumpling under my window.

That is a word I have not said;
It lies in my head
But I speak it not.
The sea teaches me
To remember quietly

What my tongue has forgot.
Father is a word my tongue once said;
Now it knows other names instead.

Father, father, remembers the sea,
Quietly under my window.

DIALOGUE

You're like a still pool in the rocks, he told her,
You hear the thudding of a surf far off.
You feel the surging of the sea's mountains
Up and down the long green mountain pathways
Only as a bright and silver ripple
Of a fish swimming somewhere. Wake up, he cried,
And move with the fierce motion of the sea.
She shifted her feet under her, as a pool does, softly.
See this red pebble?—I love red ones, she said.

WARNING

I have a sea to lie on, deep as breathing,
Swept as a wave unbreaking in its rise.
The silver foam of oat seed blown and wreathing
Rides in a smother of waters on my eyes.

Should you come down the green hill behind me,
Searching lightly, walking the hidden ground,
Breath deep under the grass tops you would find me,
Unquestionably drowned.

SEA-WIND

Yours is a wind even the beanfields bend before.
Branches that smell of sky
Lean with a creaking sigh under its lofty blowing,
Under its passing by.

Grass in the marsh bends its lean back to the salt wet,
To the bitter frost.
And the black tossed heads of rushes lifting to the sunlight
Break and are lost.

Stones on the hill shrug up their shoulders stiffened and cold.
You will not be content
With boughs rent out of heaven forever and ever,
With stones bent.

Your wind will come out of the high places and pathways
To the dust's dim core.
Leaf by leaf, silver and small, yours is a wind
The beanfields bend before.

TO A METAPHYSICAL AMAZON

If you had world more durable to walk on,
Would your quick heels
Still earnestly construct a firmer pavement
Than any street reveals?

And still impatient of appearances
Would you deride
The soft earth with the loud reality
Of your hard stride?

Ours is a world intensely insecure,
Yet proud indeed
To have performed so long and patiently
Service not guaranteed.

Might you not then accept this modest ground
For its brief worth,
Tempering the sound of heels that can
Create a stronger earth?

AFTER THIS, SEA

This is as far as the land goes, after this it is sea.
This is where my father stopped, being no sailor;

Being no Beowulf nor orient-spice hungry,
Here he let horizons come quietly to rest.

What he fled was past and over,
Raftered roof and quilted cover,
The known street and the known face,
The stale place.

This is as far as the land goes, here we are at bay,
Facing back on the known street and roof, all flight
Spent before our birth in building the new towns,
Letting these last horizons come quietly to rest.

We have a special pressing need,
We of this outer border breed,
To climb these hills we cannot flee,
To swim in this sea.

This is as far as the land goes, here the coast ranges
Soft and brown stand down to hold the ocean.
Here the winds are named for saints and blow on leaves
Small, young, yellow, few, but bound to be ancestral.

Nowhere are so still as here
Four horizons, or so clear.
Whatever we make here, whatever find,
We cannot leave behind.

ON INHABITING AN ORANGE

All our roads go nowhere.
Maps are curled
To keep the pavement definitely
On the world.

All our footsteps, set to make
Metric advance,
Lapse into arcs in deference
To circumstance.

All our journeys nearing Space
Skirt it with care,
Shying at the distances
Present in air.

Blithely travel-stained and worn,
Erect and sure,
All our travels go forth,
Making down the roads of Earth
Endless detour.

DEFINITION

Stars are food for the fed—
That is their place.
For them the surfeited
Softly say grace.

For them eyes open wide,
Lips quickly part,
And they have satisfied
The rich in heart.

To the warmed they are chill, they are dim
To the unforgot.
They are silver bread to him
Who hungers not.

PHYSIOLOGUS

When the mind is dark with the multiple shadows of facts,
There is no heat of the sun can warm the mind.
The facts lie streaked like the trunks of trees at evening,
Without the evening hope that they may find
Absorbent night and blind.

Howsoever sunset and summer bring rest
To the rheumatic by change, and howsoever
Sulphur's good medicine, this can have no cure—
This weight of knowledge dark on the brain is never
To be burnt out like fever,

But slowly, with speech to tell the way and ease it,
Will sink into the blood, and warm, and slowly
Move in the veins, and murmur, and come at length
to the tongue's tip and the finger's tip most lowly,
And will belong to the body wholly.

from

Lines at Intersection

1939

HERALD

Delivers papers to the doors of sleep,
Tosses up news upon the shores of sleep
In the day's damp, in the street's swamp wades deep
And is himself the boy drowned, drowned with sleep.

Crosses to the corner with the lamp
Already dark, even asleep with the lamp,
Treads in the wet grass, wares, leaps as in swamp
The gutters dark with darkening of the lamp.

Hears only the thud and thud against the doors
Of the news falling asleep against the doors,
The slip and drip of mist on the two shores,
Sees without light or sight the coasts of doors.

Sees at a door a light, Herald, Sir?
Wakes to the whistle and light, Herald, Sir?
To the latch lifted and the face's blur
Wakes; wakes coin, day, greeting, Herald, Sir.

FIT

It was time to come to life, this could be understood
By the thinking sounds in the shrubbery, the clipped and airy
Sounds of scissors.

Long before the head could lift itself to listen
To the restored amplification of conversation,
The sounds of scissors

Sheared in among the branches, water ran in the trenches,
In dew upon the lawn where the mower had gone,
The sheer sound spreading.

This was the orient work in the hour slipping dark
To trim the day green to full and clean
By cut and corner,

That at crack of the clipped stalk one who came out to walk,
Pressed to assume reason, should see it in its season
In shape and flower.

$7,500

I cannot tell you what a bargain this is,
Built at a cost of seven thousand, selling
For seven five, and all utilities
In, and trees.

Landscaped front and back, strings up for lawn,
Tiled, wrought-iron fixtured, entrance hall
With an echo, echo, echo, beamed ceiling,
And a Southern feeling.

Marvelous in this spring month, in this empty field,
Out of already forgotten hammers, hands compressed,
So like a snowdrop sprung, white, delicate, and new,
With mountain view.

SOLO

The structure of music as an art behind that morning glory
Behind that oak door is perpetually refounded,
Sets to in the fresher hours toward recognition,
Is this I, and is astounded.

The bar laborious rises above the breadman's whistle,
It is I, it is music written and revealed.
In the half step and broken note, am I wrong? no, it is I,
Loud though concealed.

In this eventual song, this etude, this caprice Viennois
Is not a mountain, not a wind or breath, not a morning glory or door,
Yet hear in the way it is piling up it is sometimes I
That the keys are climbing for.

I swear it will win through the kimono sleeves and the street's ply,
By whatever chances music is surprised,
And will set up in the vines, along the wind, sound that is I,
Founded and recognized.

SEER

The psychic metaphysician sat tight in the white
Shine of the rocks outside Riverside,
It was like living in a world of mirrors
The left-hand rocks and leaves so took the light,
The left of cornflakes in the kitchenette
So took the light.

Is it wind or is it a new year, asked the psychic metaphysician
Resting his hand upon the parlor chair, and the flare
Of answers long lying in that dust dazzled him,
The left-hand cups and mirrors so took the light,
It was like living in a world of answers
The hand so took the light.

I shall be prodigal with thine information
The psychic metaphysician knelt and spelt,
Changing fifty cents to forty on his sign,
It swung against the porch and took the light,
It was like living in a world of sight
The sign so took the light.

JOSHUA

Forty miles from Arquilla, and that town
Was forty from Red Sand where the bars were
Of one kind and another, and that town
Was forty from Shell Crosscut and the depot,
A man was walking over toward the mountains,
Keeping his head down.

His name was Joshua.
Mountains might tumble down, he was a redeemer,
Heart of rock be gold and give sign of it,
Open nearer, lean out and see Joshua.
He went slanting across that open space all day without stopping,
Brush bruising and mending in his tracks in a hurry
After him.

Keeping his head down,
Keeping his arms out against the stumble of the devil,
And his face for all of landmarks in one direction;
Car going by on the through highway, he would hear,

He would stop and grow in that place for that necessary number
  of instants,
He would deceive but for the sake of the mission
And the promise, ye.

LARK

Lark hit us in the face with his rising sound.
We were unstruck by wind before and raced
Train, and saw all signs with one eye only,
And were shelled against sky
And all that we went by.

Now lark said something in the field and we heard it,
And it mounted and rode upon our ears as we sped.
And we heard windshield rattle and canvas creak thereafter,
And pondered every line
Of hill and sign.

TEHACHAPI SOUTH

Tehachapi south down with dust in the mouth
And hills that spin under wheels,
Wild lilac gray, and sunflowers sick of the sun,
And the grade run.

Faint in the ears like a shout the shifting of gears
High on the grade behind, and ahead
Easing out on the road that takes again
The smooth speed of the plain.

The earth bent up into folds yellow and spent
Now passes in pale grass
To a new horizon, farther and more neat,
Cut clean with heat.

The round high pipes following low ground,
Lying apart, bear at heart
Water, water, for men's throats. And the breath
Of the town is in the teeth.

ENTRY

Come, shall we come out of the listening season into the city,
Out of the confidential forest, the undecided bloom
Into the noncommittal
Metropolitan room.

Fifth and Main, for instance, does not put forth leaves,
It is an intersection that keeps to itself alone,
Cement having just that much more
Corner reserve than stone.

There is less, for instance, of blowing wherever listeth
And being numberless. Counter, office, car
Know to the decimal where they are going
And where they are.

There is more, for example, of the clean-cut heroic and durable,
The street and linoleum cool after a good beating,
The seventh and eighth floors outshouldering sun
At every meeting.

Come, shall we come out of the murmurous decline of leaves,
The falling hints and windy expectation,
To city where the small matter is put down already
To depreciation.

CHAMBER OF COMMERCE

Flourish your golden shores and indolent
Sibilant acquaintance with the dove,
There is yet more of ticket to be spent
Before they reach the destiny thereof.

They will not find the dove there or the sward
Or the three maidens, but the curly fleece
And the dark pellets of the raining keeping guard
Over the sun's lease.

They will light down at the station and be lost,
All the lotus smoking like mills along the way,
They will look into faces to their cost,
They will be spent with what's uncharged to pay.

Polish your palm fronds, they will still creak,
The mocker will sing and bite at the dove's tail,
And those who keep warm under the fleece will learn to speak
Double, to no avail.

MEN FRIDAY

This water is for ships, that they cleave it,
That the grooves leap
Cleanly at the bow and clearly leave it,
As freight is borne upon the face of the deep.

This ground is for feet, that they tread it,
That commerce start
In the dust, and the feet spread it
Counter to counter, paradise to port.

Came ever out of the blue a free faring
Wind upon this strand,
It would start and wonder at the sea bearing
Keel prints, at the heel prints in the sand.

PERSONIFICATION

She will define for you in the sunny morning
The self possessed.
Where are you going (my pretty maid)?
I'm going shopping (sir) she said.
Her foot on the brake is self possessed, and it shines,
Her hand on the wheel is self possessed, and the lines
Of lapel and brim, of seam and hem
Are self possessed.

The power of keys is hers
And self possessed.
Two bits for the parking (my pretty maid),
Here is your quarter (sir) she said,
And the quarter is self possessed, see it shine,
And the shine of the palm it lies in, and the line
Of chin and throat that lift to let you note
Them self possessed.

Her heel in the gravel lot
Is self possessed.
How long will you be (my pretty maid)?
About an hour (sir) she said.
Her face in the crowd is self possessed, and shining,
Her pause on the curb is self possessed, defining
To cars and stores and stares and the sun in the morning
The self possessed.

UPON TWELVE

Now has been contrived in the increasing noonday
Some show of order wherein to be at rest,
Some stilling of the need that space be tended,
That time be pressed.

Where in our path was the ambitious clutter of morning,
The leaf shadow and stir, the brush and broom,
Now at the base of trees is a clean sunlight,
At the door, room.

We shall sit with minds quiet, with the loftiness, though cooler,
That the sun has for its meridian,
In the fine short space before the roof eastward
Darkens again.

INTERLUDE

Chorus remarks woe,
Tide comes up on the town,
Still this is lunchtime and I like milkshakes,
I like wrists rested at last on counters,
Smooth and loud the rest, the foreign flavor
Of rest foaming up roundly, misting on the mirror.
Come peach or strawberry where the bee sucks,
How hat bends over you with its little feather,
Its minor frolic, is this all for woe,
Is this to the earth's west setting and dismay?
Look then, we shall mark it up in round figures,
15¢ register and be done with it,

And by that token so record delight,
So scientifically score it,
Chorus cannot ignore it.

DAY

I never saw a sky like this since twenty-three,
This is a bluer top to the town than men look for,
It is a miracle and they close their eyes at it.

> What do the frogs do in the dingle?
> They speak as if we had a moon.
> What do the trees do? They abandon shadow
> And father noon.

In twenty-three we had a sky on this order,
The stone under the faucet bleached out in that weather
And has got no moss yet in memory of it.

> What do the gnats do? They so report the sun,
> They so relay messages of wire import
> That the wires themselves are quiet
> And shine short.

Not often do you see four edges all together,
And sky of such blue corner at Saunder's very drugstore.
It is a day of a nature to remember about.

DRIVER SAYING

Lady hold your horses, sit down in your seat,
Wrap your feet around the leg of the chair,
Even in my heart I can feel your heart beat.

We move, however, on schedule of need
Of the general public, see, standing on the corner there,
Holding hats, lifting canes, cutting down our speed.

Lady calm down, we'll be stopping and starting
On your nerves and my brakes ten corners more,
There'll be plenty feet to watch climbing up and departing.

There is also a good signboard at the Filmart
To look at and keep your mind on when we pass there.
Lady, even in second I can hear your heart.

APPROACH

The hosiery salesman walking up the hill
Holds out for mercy and receives it not,
Perceiving at the top against his will
How flat the blocks ahead are and how hot.

How from porch to porch and hedge to hedge
In neo-Spanish neatness of design
There is a long perspective of arch and edge
Of roof and step and little out of line.

These doors will close to his toe one like the rest,
The cool interiors be black to his sight,
No eager discourse on what silk is best
Will sound in his ears right.

How shall a man proceed among the noises
Of scooters, rakes, and babies on the lawn
When the sober Spanish doors and the cool voices
Reject all small familiars but their own?

CALCULATION

We have within our sky an orbit taken
By Greenwich time,
The larger orders of the stars forsaken.

Rising in afternoon and setting due
South in two minutes or thereabout thereafter,
This body has no dark or light ensue,

But makes in its regular coursing unstellar hum,
Marking by sound, by heavier silence after,
The way that it has come.

QUESTION

One watched the face listening and thinking of questions,
What it would answer it labored for.
The shadow of thought moved softly over it.

It said this: I do not know.
And one was wearied with following after,
And glad of reply achieved so hardly.

THE FAITH

Sir, take this faith, it will do you no harm.
It is mine and sits on your shoulder.
It will not chatter.

It will take pleasure in seeing you move,
You are hesitant and placid and that is a good motion,
And faith is a good devotion.

Sir, do not refuse one's stranger companiment,
It will insist by no sign or pressure
And will have measure.

ENLIGHTENMENT

I wish we could take a statistic with more grace, beloved,
I wish it would circle out in our minds to the very brim,
And we could be illumined by data one by one, as by candles,
As by the cheerful faces of cherubim.

But see, we respond only to archangelic doctrine,
Look up and glow at the actual pronouncement of grace,
Swallow at once all the high-powered radiance,
And let the commandments shine upon the face.

This is a tremendous lot of revelation we gather,
Beloved, and beam at it in the proper spirit.
Nevertheless I wish we had one or two facts to go by,
And a less arc-lighted kingdom to inherit.

PASSION

Hobbes spoke among the ball cries, telling what
Was passion.
In the sixth inning, the interior beginning
Of voluntary motion.

Bat crack and book debate were underblent,
Though blocked apart,
Moving together from eyes, ears, and other
Organs to the heart.

ROOTER

Played ball yourself once, mister?
Once, yes. No talker mister.
Picks up no stray balls, makes no remark,
Sticks around till dark.

Cold afternoons with the sun fading
Yardline the street with the trees' shading.
On fields so hard the scores run
Higher and hotter than the sun.

Audience watches hit the bat,
In an overcoat and a gray hat,
Deep his hands in his pockets, tense;
Stilled by the shouting, the audience.

The tree where he leaned not warm to touch,
The grass not trodden very much,
The curb where he stood as cold as stone
In the dark, when he is gone.

FOR FUTURES

When the lights come on at five o'clock on street corners
That is Evolution by the bureau of power,
That is a fine mechanic dealing in futures:
For the sky is wide and warm upon that hour.

But like the eyes that burned once at sea bottom,
Widening in the gloom, prepared for light,
The ornamental standards, the glazed globes softly
Perceive far off how probable is night.

ROW

Some of the roofs are of Hopi Indian decision,
They cut square into the sky with plaster,
The tan edge going up two stories past the windows
And turning north and east for straight cement horizon.

Some have old noble English temper peaked,
Alternate red and green shingles but getting the drift,
Gabled to peer out of a possible anciently fallen snow,
And clear superior against gray sky.

All of them look west and take in sunset,
Keep their ferns warm the length of supper,
Sparkle their cups of milk and all accompany
With aerial music that evening sun go down.

PREMIERE

The searchlights ask the stars nothing
Among them going,
Tell them nothing, their sign of show
Being for more particular sight below.

Show, show, say they to the sight
Through the lamplight,
Raying cloud, cloud, and cloud to wake and start
The after-dinner heart.

There is stir in the driveways and rustle of departing,
With the hearts starting,
And sight can almost see, ear hear, at the lights' core
Gathering, shining, what the lights are searching for.

LIGHT YEAR

If you had one more swirl you would have a good haircut,
Prosper Prosper.
If you had one more curl you would be a lady,
Prosper.
Why did you buy that flat brown hat?
You look like yourself in that.
What do I look like, what do I look like,
Prosper?

One more mile and you will wind up in Jericho,
Prosper Prosper.
One mile more over the Ninety-ninth Street bridge,
Prosper.
What is that tower on the left by the gasworks?
This isn't the place for looking at landmarks.
Drive it or sell it, drive it or sell it,
Prosper.

If we had one more hat we should look like an army,
Prosper Prosper.
If we had one more headlight, a fire engine,
Prosper.
How many lights in a mile from here?
How many miles in a light year?
This is a light year, this is a light year,
Prosper.

CAT

Lady in the leopard skin
Has a fear of plunging in
Traffic like a muddy river,
Starting gives a little shiver.

Gears and peers and fears again
That her horn is not too plain,
Edges to curb, pauses to think
How to move upon the brink.

Go ahead, implores the tender,
Heavy-handed on the fender,
In her ears the engine sings
Yellow-eyed, the lady springs.

THE DIRECTORS

See the roofs bend down at behest of moving picture,
We are in montage up to plain omniscience,
The plot pieced, set to be sung and acted in,
And we act in it.

See the trees bend to the reel of moving picture,
The road unwind like plot not neat but nimbly,
The roofs come in, in crowd of complication:
We know the ending.

Not guess what goes behind the hundred windows
Or in the hundred trees that crack the curbstone,
But take it all up into plot and call it
Coming attraction.

We are in simple silence of excitement
Seeing the night unwind as we direct it,
Moving, under impress of moving picture,
Plot into morrow.

MADE SHINE

This face had no use for light, took none of it,
Grew cavernous against stars, bore into noon
A dark of midnight by its own resources.

Yet where it lay in sleep, where the pillows held it
With the blind plaster over it and the four walls
Keeping the night carefully, it was undone.

Sixty-watt light, squared to a window frame,
Across a well of air, across wind and window
Leaped and made shine the dark face in its sleep.

CENTER

What they had at their window was earth's own shadow,
What they had on their garden, bloom's intermission,
Slept in the car the graceful far.

Slept in the breast a city and statewide rest,
Ran at the wrist time strapped and glassed,
They had eyes closed tight in a central standard night.

MEANING MOTION

Alarm smites upon the covers, clenches the hands,
Their own voices saying six o'clock have now turned tin,
Have now turned back upon the night and cut within,
And slippers and slid blankets without dawn the day begin.

    Ah, the striped flannel and the peach blossoms
    Arise into the day
    In disarray.

Soap slips from them, though grimed or jellied, fresher,
Steam roars in pipes if it is home this morning,
Eyes lift and wake and lift, to mirror turning,
Through mist of breath and hair tossed set to learning.

    Ah, the clean faces and the beards lost
    Waken to peer the day
    In glass display.

The crisp and bitter warm them, cups their fingers,
Breaking the fast of news and thought and telling
How crust tastes, how France fares, how rails are selling,
And by what means Moon Mullins is compelling.

    Ah, the white shirtsleeves and the shirtmaker
    Recall from far away
    Procedures of the day.

Door sticks to take the key but is made fast.
They are remembering the day and its content,
And on the tracks and walks what way they went,
And time and fortune, how firmly they are spent.

Ah, the pressed suits, they waken on the day,
In recalled array
They have taken on the day.

from

Poems on Several Occasions

1941

MARKET REPORT ON COTTON GRAY GOODS

Cotton gray goods quiet and firmer
Sold in small amounts at steady prices.
Some were unaware at distance from the market
How those bolts reflected prepossessed their cost per head
And quieted.

Raw silk was unchanged and rayon yarns actively
Lapped up demand that firmed to cream just,
Rose with time just topping at the market,
A calm waylaying and surrendering, a portion sped
And quieted.

Wool goods mills started showing suitings,
Bustled up a test drama of art and taste,
The higher life at slightly higher prices
Suggested by an exact at-homeness of stripe, bred
And quieted.

After luncheon the stocks prevailed further
In a muted influence and exercise of will
Tanging the office airs like manifests
Of season, which they were, unfolding spread
And quieted.

Conveyed not only crop but moon quarter,
State of mortgage, not only ground but floor
Of wage, put over to mind the color of climate,
Fence-rail and stool both, corn and boughten bread,
Yet quieted.

Conveyed, so listening was that atmosphere, a dry
Air that comes seldom at seaboard but then has absorbed
A catalogue of some possible warm accents and beliefs,
Conveyed warp brought to grief and packing rioted
Yet quieted.

Quieted in the streets of afternoon the dry interior air,
Occasioning a steadying of burlap in the late day,
Through the good offices of the rolls themselves
Their own substantial nature weaved and undersaid
And quieted.

COMMITTEE REPORT ON SMOKE ABATEMENT IN RESIDENTIAL AREA

Prevailing winds in this area blow
The fume of life away.
The mesh-bag carriers when they go to shop
Can look around the day.

A ceiling blue maintains a working breath
Of ozone in the street,
And blinds blow inward with a birdy note
Of sun complete.

However, three or four months out of the year
Prevailing winds abate,
And the smoke of interest enters
Closet however strait.

Today is such a one. Some off in the smoke
Keep the miles dim.
And some at home bake black enough for the
  kids when they get there
Bread of the brothers Grimm.

GOVERNMENT INJUNCTION RESTRAINING HARLEM COSMETIC CO.

They say La Jac Brite Pink Skin Bleach avails not,
They say its Orange Beauty Glow does not glow,
Nor the face grow five shades lighter nor the heart
Five shades lighter. They say no.

They deny good luck, love, power, romance, and inspiration
From La Jac Brite ointment and incense of all kinds,
And condemn in writing skin brightening and whitening
And whitening of minds.

There is upon the federal trade commission a burden of glory
So to defend the fact, so to impel
The plucking of hope from the hand, honor from the complexion,
Sprite from the spell.

THE SAME

Mercedes was the lady's name and she had in her voice
A batch of tunes to tell the day how it was doing.
Often about eleven she would start one after another
Very silently, and come to no conclusion.

Afternoon, though, the day could stop any time,
Break up its traffic, bid its criers peace,
Seize the miraculous instant, and hear tuned
Under Royal keys what Mercedes thought of it.

APPOINTMENT IN DOCTOR'S OFFICE

The lady put off her fur, it was so warm in the outer office,
She was pale but not because she was frightened. She was afraid.
She looked at the framed pictures, particularly one of mountains
with sunlight,
Then she got out her glasses and read *Harper's Bazaar*
In which was a striking teaset of cream and jade.
She smoothed her gloves because whe was afraid.

The lady would not look at the little boy waiting in the outer
office,
Because he kept his hands together and did not smile.
She would not look at the one who held him,
Reminding him at intervals not to cry.
And yet thereafter she did reassuringly smile
For what was evidently a long while.

The lady sat with her little broken bone and thought about Hawaii,
Now and again stopping and taking breath.
Every chair was filled with the smoke of waiting,
The pages turning in intense parlor atmosphere,
Till when at the long long long overdue beckon she took breath
The lady was sick unto death.

BEACH PARTY GIVEN BY T. SHAUGHNESSY FOR THE SISTERS

Seven nuns went wading in the sea,
They wore no shoes,
They lined up along the shore and the shore washed out
And flooded back to the very knee.
A rough but good shore and sea.

The seaweed and the wimple habits were,
Close and alive,
Both cumbrous but of will designed and worn.
For every nun the sea was good to her,
And alike their habits were.

It was so rough a day, like cormorants more
You would have thought
The nuns would take to nest, but still they cried and stayed.
They were like to the devout sea, and to the shore
They sisters were.

PEAK ACTIVITY IN BOARDWALK HAM CONCESSION

What was that they heard past the peal
Of the booth's bells and the squeal
Round the turned edges of the wide red sucker?
Past the surf of the game wheel
The surf of ocean.

> Here's your hot ham folks, tells
> To the peal of the booth's bells,
> To the round red face round the red sucker,
> The driven voice that spells
> Ham to the ocean.

What was that the licker heard
That her tongue slow on the third
Round tasted there more of salt than strawberry sucker,
Marking without a word
The lick of ocean?

> Here's the turn of the wheel folks, cries
> To the wheel's fall and rise,

To the fall of dimes and the face of the all-day sucker,
The driven voice to the rise
And fall of ocean.

POLO MATCH. SUNDAY, 2 P.M.

Polo is that gravy-look game,
Tough brushed out and thus adaptable,
Rare, but thick and springy,
Thought up as a grist well chewed by a good tooth.

The soppers of that gravy save all Sunday for it
And picnic at its bounds; they sit on Sunday papers
And pay no fee but the warning distant gasp
Of the multitude so good for a good pony.

Polo picks up an area of turf and takes it
Right down the lines, it biases the natural green,
It goals the very day, with evidence
Of practice flavoring that efficiency.

Riders have the watchers licking chops,
Not only in the pleased way of relatives and friends,
But in the ready gust of the professional eaters
Taking the taste up deftly from a distance.

Gravy, gravy of the haunch and flexion
Sliding and righting, at a chewable degree
Soaks down the Sunday aft in a feast for the breadwinners,
The breadwinners winning it all up deep to saturation.

COMMITTEE DECISION ON PECANS FOR ASYLUM

Orphans are to have, instead of walnuts
From a state two thousand and twenty miles distant,
Pecans from home.

The Santa Claus committee up and authorized
One ton of back walnuts for the orphan stockings
But found ton bottom bad.

Took the word of the agricultural inspectors
Somebody had been led on a bad buy
Pulling the whiskers of the jolly saint.

Tossed out the lying samples suitable and savory,
Eligible for orphans, and acknowledged
Better pecans from home.

Orchards of home, the orphan house and home own,
Sweeten in the cold for their first hard teeth,
The fluted sweet brittle and home-grown
Substance in sheath.

Kernels of home, frosting with Christmas cheer,
Crispen not for an individual mantel and tongue
But a massed patriot lunge and lick this year,
The hungry younger democrat so does long.

Shake out intending crackle over that brisk brick,
Making to matron and minor mildly known
How under the burnish and the bluff of stick
The sweet is grown.

The committee saint withdraws the possibility
Of a foreign exotic flavor for the ribs,
Of black nut crack,

And goes back of necessity to its original and time-tried
Local lesson of the nature of good
Pecans from home.

ART GALLERY CLOSING TIME

Steps never went away so far as when they carried
Mr. and Mrs. Smith out of the gallery of the museum of art.
Steps went down out of morning and one could not turn round
and ascend them.

They went down into evening out of the gallery of the palace
of art
And so brought one into Mr. MacGregor's chaos,
A fine thriving city with car tracks and stop signs every which
way.

They went out into the red network of evening,
One white marble portion after another nimbly rounding
Away from the morning marshes and flamingoes in the palace
of the legion of art.

NOW THAT APRIL'S HERE

Coming up to the boulevard stop on the slant,
The poplars standing off along,
The white proceeding and as white crossed,
One would have to look a west sun in the eye.

Picking up after La Cienega the long quiet,
The porch lights flying, still as they are.
The cars staying along the curb north and south quiet,
One would have to go straight chin deep in light on the level
tracts.

Stopping for ice, bouncing in short against the red paint,
The store building facing up like a bastille,
One would have to get breath to look off down the street,
Down the low roofs, races of pavement, meadows of evening.

And so I would if there I were, there I would take
One into another the long flat avenues of the angels,
Lower than the west light, the luminous levels,
There through the shiny shallows remember that one dimension.

THE LIGHTING OF THE STREETLIGHTS

Corinthian is the light they see by,
It renews Corinth in the fall of blue,
Polishing the car tops and the carob trees
In marble custom and the linear shade.

When they run out to get ice cream it is the light that shines over them,
Fluted in length; illumines
The face of the mantel clock when no one asks the time,
Abides that round of dark over them.

It is white on pedestal in classic vein
In the first pitching of morning when they come home elate,
Column burning with a cool ancient flare,
The light they see by, the Corinthian.

THE LIGHTING OF A SMALL FIRE IN THE GRATE

When oak is burning, that is warming
At earth's fire, grown up in wood and established.
What when
Newspaper stews and fizzles in the grate?

That, let a Barrymore conclude, is a wet humanity,
A print of a thousand feet and eyes, all damp
But lit
To keep a spirit flaring at its heat.

That is history not yet a wood, but a good
Pulp nipping at the flame, a personal endeavor
Of persons in the news
To serve and blaze.

MODERN DANCE PROGRAM: AMERICAN DOCUMENT

God how we gallop, the youth of the land,
Every shoulder Atlas atlastic,
Sleuthing slowly and of sudden hurray, enthus-
Iastic.

Gropers to grow for tension of toe
Patristic,
Natal brittle mental metal and fatal-
Istic.

With stile, smile, and piano there is possibly
A picnic,
But definitely youth muscle and what you may call it, and
  definitely tech-
Nic.

PRELIMINARY
TO CLASSROOM LECTURE

My quiet kin, must I affront you
With a telling tongue?
Will not a mission or request content you
To move as you belong
The fields of doubt among?

The voice to burden down a tale upon you
Were indolent with din.
Would better ask and have the answer from you.
And would you then begin
Querying too, querying, my quiet kin?

PURCHASE OF
LODGING FOR THE NIGHT

Evil hemmed the curtains and swung in with them slightly
When slightly the western air blew in.
Evil starched the pillow, it was evil
So firmly feathered.

Tourist from high road came in and put his bag down,
Washed his face, read his magazine,
And there came evil numbering the page twenty,
Singing in the light bulb.

All night turned when he turned, looked across the mirror,
Crowed at cock-crow,
But lay still in the linoleum and hem of curtain
When he went down to breakfast.

PURCHASE OF
HAT TO WEAR IN THE SUN

Sombrero is comfort because it keeps thought under foot,
Keeps the personal shadow to heel,
Keeps the stride covered,
Covers brain cosily from reel.

Paces along in a degree of sun put to it
To force hard, and under, the addle pate,
And yet filters all that compulsion
Compelled to its own colonial gait.

Provides the porch of shade and colonnade for thought
To rock in, surveying the domain not too continuously,
And steadies spot of domain out of sun,
Even where's none other to survey.

Tips the sombrero on, the mortal booted,
And travels under it, thinking
Just enough coolly and in shadow
To survive under blessing without blinking.

PURCHASE OF A BLUE, GREEN, OR ORANGE ODE

Jake's store past Pindaric mountain
Over the wash is the only place in a day's ride
To get odes at except close to Mesa City side.

He has one glass a dusty one there
Full of blue green and orange odes sticky but OK,
And many come by on that account that way.

Scramble down off the hot flats, swallow a lot of universal wind,
Hear that lone freight pushing around sandy acre,
And they need for the slow swipes one green jawbreaker.

A slug of sweet, a globe of a barber's pole,
A suck of a human victory out of a crowd,
Sugared, colored, out of a jar, an ode.

Early Uncollected Poems

1940s-60s

IMPERATIVE

Of yourself, and of that only
Softly and without thought,
Talk, for I am tired of talk and lonely.

This unregarded murmuring, and this
Unanswerable voice
Will make a peace more warm than silence is.

PROGRAM

Martin on every block
Is in luck.
Here's time for belt-buckling.
What music says so?

> The stained-glass organ raining down
> Its pelts over noon-town?
> Maybe.
>
> The tooter at the bridge, puffer in the bay,
> Bird in the marsh at payday?
> Maybe.
>
> The tyke balloon bargains, staying away from the pins
> They promise you, till the waft begins.
> Maybe so.
>
> The coming together at the goal line which means to press,
> The full-tide roar of a major success?
> Maybe yes.
>
> The natural sounds of far-out foreigners,
> Brook water, wave washes, wind whisks and such stirs?
> Yes again.

These airs in the block, what they carry amazes
To each his own traces.
Does one single one ever hear all these musics?
Maybe, Maybe so.

HEAD IN HANDS

When a man's hands take his hair close at the skull,
At head center at the dark root and pull,
Then he is pulling at his heavy wit
To waken it.

Crying in pain of will and wristbone deep
To the long schools of memory where they keep.
See how the hands would draw
A science to the brow.

HIGHROAD

The coast highway at our grade occasioned
Every night in its middle when the fields were dumb
An over-excessive parleying of engines,
Plaints
Like remonstrance.

The trucks prepared to climb, and the road responded,
Four-laned and loud in every lane,
To the change quick and the recognition.
It was quite
A rally and a quarrel in the night.

We in our beds now are not so taken
Up into the story in sleep, because the tanks
Don't pause or change, the trundle's unintermittent,
We'd as well
Live on a level.

GRAVITY

We were losing altitude all the time,
We were coming down fast under the leaves of trees,
We sat and let the steep street pull us down.
    There was no more sun upon these sidewalks,
    Though the air was thick with sun where we had been.
    The ground was rough with stone on top of the hill:
    Here it was green.

When we slowed out of the wind we could hear voices
Playing games somewhere all by themselves;
And the streetlights went on because we came to them.
    We shall be watched over, we who have come back
    To the level, under the green leaves of the tree,
    With the brakes on, touching the curb, breathlessly saying
    All outs in free.

ROMANTIC LETTER

Dear Jo, Margaret has been taken
To Tehachapi prison in the green June,
In the summer that is here.
She will be a bird-in-cage,
She will have a raven rage.
The pickers in the little summer valleys
Will trade the peaches for the twenty cents,
And Margaret will lean her head and cry.
The softest prison breath will be her sigh
For the pennies they have not, for the warriors forgot,
For the cause not won or lost enough to die.
It is war she will wage in the pamphlet on the page.
Dreaming of her pickers in the still of summertime,
In the still of air of crime.
Jo, I think that I must write this all,
I will do a ballad of grief
And of loss, but of rising
And of Margaret, what she said.
I will give up Guinevere in the play I wrote you of,
After all, she is dead.
There is Margaret instead, and the front of criminal
Syndicalism.   Beth, with love.

MINES, EXPLOSIONS

Mines, explosions, and collisions
Conducted themselves with expedition
Over the globe, in the still water,
At the sandy banks, in the coral shoals,
At the lime cliff, in the bath-capped surf

Achieved existence and an actual fame.
    How did they manage? What is success?

Mines, explosions, and collisions
Had their pictures in the evening editions
Over the globe, on the glassy bottoms,
In the turfy seas, in the peaty channels
Made their way, though some of their men were rescued.
Made their way with ardor and impression.
    Who were their associates? What is success?

Mines, explosions, and collisions
Must have some friends and multiple connections,
Candid contacts, pride, and personal honors.
I never knew any, I never was
Traveled on those shores and bathing seas, I wonder
Who so traveled, who aided and who knew them,
    Who were their friends? What is success?

MARKET

Three minutes after the fuehrer spoke
To the bending ears in the marketplace, Souls
Said the fuehrer, the fading followed
In wheat, faded.

All peace, peace the shortwaves spoke
In their own obedient job recording exactly Souls
So that the wheat hearts grew sick at heart and swallowed
Convulsively and sank.

One and seven eighths lower for what he spoke
That was the factor in fleeting downward, Souls
Honestly making no discounts for irony and bellowed
Defenses as of pay.

The wheat believed the peace for what it spoke
And knew wheatena mission small for Souls
Who would be furnished with peace pomegranate and pillow,
Knew its position mediocre.

Wheat hearts the golden-haired lapsed along as the fuehrer spoke
And dewed with tears of mournfully unwarring Souls

Reflected faithfully the blister of peace as it hallowed.
Flared fresh and faded.

In notable sympathy corn, rye, and oats after he spoke
Without parley took their cue from wheat, and the bent Souls
Listening in the marketplace past words heard hollowed
The swept grainy rustle of decline.

ABSOLUTE MAN

The best to say for a hard-bitten man
With a cleft chin is
His will's in the right direction.

He doesn't blow cold and crow
Blow hot and cry
But goes and again goes in the same direction.

The absolute man he is
With a nose for an east breeze
And one ear mossy ever.

LYRIC

Oil is what I have for you,
Oil for you,
I have that black gold seeping up through the sands
For you.

Where the countries of Roosevelt, Hyde, and Samper come together
In Texas, in east Texas that is called
The triangle strip,
Where the Red River and the Little Brother come together
Down there flowing in the oil-bearing rock land,
Take that trip

And stand there with the Great American Oil Company
Out to your left where the sun is going down,
See their towers lighted.
And stand there with the Paladin on your right hand
Pumping heart out of the ground so busy,
Their shifts doubled and yields kited.

Feel under your heels, feel oil at work ready
To be yours to barrel in your stock and pour your cup full
As they say.
You will ask, you hardhead from Missouri and I don't blame you,
What about Great American and Paladin in this business,
Where are they?

They are out, that is the answer, this is privately owned land,
Privately owned for you, and keeps the business representatives
Of the big boys tearing their hair,
Champing on the banks of the Red and Little Brother
While you go in and take up your own acre
And draw your own private American fortune there.

I have oil for you.
Your oil man has that message and you are Garcia.
Oil-rich luxury flowing from the triangle of the state of Texas
For you.

PELLEAS AND MELISANDE

George, I am convinced I know what I want.
I know how to get it, there is advertising,
I will advertise.
I want a farmer with muscles, George,
And I want a farm girl
With hazel eyes.
I want the simple stuff like blue jeans, George,
Chromium piffle and clear all this stuff out,
I've got the groove.
I am entirely off the Scarlett type, the Violet type, the
    blues type, George,
I want the taffy kind.
I want somebody for the people to love.

My boy, we need creation in this country,
We need the simple people recognized
And brought alive,
The sturdy glamour of the country drugstore,
The hearty glamour of gingham and suspenders,
The simple glamour of the two for five.

My boy give me my hat, I'm walking on air,
I see on the screen the shine of the simple faces,
The pretty hazel eyes.
A white horse too, George, and a country farmhand
Riding,
One of those gold-hearted guys.

I'll talk to Mr. Steinhart about this
And we'll fix up the campaign, we'll comb the farms,
Every fence will carry the news,
We're looking for a chance for a new romance,
The times are just ripe for the happy type,
We're through with the blues.

VERDICT

It suffers by the jurist,
It pales at the count,
At the reckoning of amount.
It is by mercy,
By not asking why;
It is driven to die
By the reasonable reply.
We are fixed on law,
We are eloquent by reason.
We act not out of season.
What shall we do with the unaccountable,
With the unconvictable, we
Being the jury?

DINNER BELL

We have got one word like a dinner bell without any clapper
And that is peace. At evening and at noon
The lumbermen from the branches of forests,
Hardies from the sea, Dr. Smith,
Postman and thief, none of these come and get it,
Nobody hears that bell a-ringing.

The cooks have to make a more than usual attempt,
Use washboards with a stick and tubs to beat on,
Make the array of cookery itself
Proclaim the possibility of being fed,
And douse the little bell and holler out
Soup's on the stove, supper itself a-ringing.

SALESMAN

Man came into the Grill selling business papers,
Asked for the manager.
I was warming up a pot of coffee, took my time,
Walked over and gave him the kind of day.

Got no manners from him except his hat off.
He took that off
Looking in the mirror past the cereal stack,
A straight looker at his own bare face.

He sold me a short line, picked up his stuff,
Picked up
That big look, put his hat on it,
Took it away.

DEC. 7, 1941

On the war day, mainly the soldiers got going.
Around some corners with which I was familiar
The steps were still mostly up and down,
Meditative, and not widely directed.

The little wars still raged, of crutch with stair,
Beard with crumb, buyer with incantation,
Trouble with peace, the awkwardest
Fights, and freest of origin.

VOTER

How much is an old man
A citizen?
An old alone old man
Breathing now and then?

Well, he walks on every morning
In the approaching sun
And uses up more of it
Than most people can.

He goes all over,
Sees little done,
His eye cloudy
And his sense unplain.

And casts his vote, if a vote defines
A citizen
All down the line, back to 'eighty, to Adam,
Before most begin.

The man he votes for being fuller
Than anyone
Suspects of patience, age, policy
And sun.

CONVERSATION

Some people talk nothing for four or a hundred
But language for two.
Quips.
Special beruffled style. Do you get it?
You are not supposed to.

Adornment taps the Morse dashes and the sender
Laughs neatly,
Quips.
That was a good one. Do you get it? Wait,
Sometimes he will translate it to you.

WARDEN

Send me a voice from the store.
I stop
Under a leaf-letting tall tree
To light
The spark to lip and keep the prospect stirring.

Such a still night, a pelt of growing grounds,
But sounds
Sheltered, conserved, enclosed.
I talk
Inside, studying on the paved road.

Buy me a big lingering line of talk then,
I'm foundered
At this post in the narrative dark
With not a whisper.
The great neighborhood bloom close as a clam.

SHIFT

Many of the bodies arose at the graveyard shift
From the literal graveyard as from the hot beds
Of the federal housing project; they bent their backs
To the war effort.

Many sinews snapped, the grandmothers
Played out soonest in the local moonlight,
Nor was a headstone any less heavy
Upon younger necks strained and retired.

The impulsion of the people's will clearly
Had got down six feet underground.
But whether any argument got down there
Mortality has not ascertained.

AND AFTER

My life is astray in the mind,
Rooted at heart, planted at foot,

Happy at hand,
And aloof and astray in the mind.

What is the whistle at lone,
The oblivious brisk and packet of past,
And the truck of the tune
In the whistle at lone?

I am deft as my neighbors and dafter
And cannot get home.
Yet live there before them and after,
Before them and after.

MAN OF COURAGE

Bartlett in his place lived fifty summers of anguish
Concealing anguish from acquaintances,
Shedding the tenderest of living smiles on these.

But his was nothing to the anguish which
Strangers noticed in their spines for him.
He was an invigorating gentleman.

SPRING '44

Nothing is so quick as a clocked robin,
But who'll clock a robin, says my sister to me,
One two three.

Nothing is so shot as a shot sparrow,
But who'd shoot a sparrow with a Garand or arrow,
Wistfully
Says my sister to me.

What is so fierce as a doubtful fighter,
Spring's at the front and the bird in the tree,
Let's be off to the wars, says my sister to me.

HORIZON

Often I think what does your goodness matter
That lives in gulfs beyond my reaching breath,
Lives in your life, not mine, will die for you
After your death.

As if on Mars, beyond feasible space travel
You came and went to work, nor left me still
Knowing of your coming and going, but to wonder
If you were well.

Then suddenly I think by recollection
How every goodness known,
Even dreamed of, even denied, is that immortal
Future we verge upon.

VIEWS TO SEE CLAYTON FROM

His brother's wife can't stand Clayton.
She's a nurse, neat and a hard worker,
And what's in Don of the radical's in him worse
And scares her more.

Don, the disk in him can be worn like leather,
She saves his life over and over
And gives it prize, polish, so they fit
Like hand in glove.

But then here's Clayton lurking about his parent's home
Looking for mischief, and a hand on his sleeve
Makes him jump. Leave him alone,
He's more trouble than we want in this world.

His father says that as a small boy
Clayton had more gumption than anyone in the family.
Nobody so quick to jump off a thirty-foot board
Into the deepest water, didn't know the name of danger.

But along about the age of discretion he must have picked some up.
Anyway from then on he always hesitated
Before he plunged off into those risks of his,
But always plunged off, coming back hurt, that's Clayton now.

His mother softly says, Clay could be a real leader.
Somewhere, how could I tell, he took not to.
He was the one with ideas, grew the garden
With the green thumb, teased the girls.
What a tease he was, softly his mother,
And still is, for that matter.

Don remembers old Clay when 69 Squadron
Flew wing to wing, given three inches
Either way the whole thing would collide,
It was his hand held those inches spaced between them,
And what a bringer, when he got off that cloud.

He was always a smart boy, Aunt Martha,
Quick, eager, couldn't put anything over on Clay.
Answering every time he got the teacher's eye,
Opinionated, but the smart are often that way.

Even cynical, you might say. How does it happen
The bright turn sour on us? It's hard to find
Of our chief leaders today any who
Showed real promise when they were young.

Damn you, Clayton, Uncle Henry says,
You're so restless, you break up everybody else's well-
earned rest.
Career down the highway, you're apt to hit somebody.
And what will we do then with the insurance money?

Damn you, Clayton, Uncle Henry says,
Your father and I have worked for maybe forty years now
To get a steady place to put our feet on,
To put your childish feet.

When they were all sitting around in the living room
I was there too, but I didn't think I should say very much,
So I listened. How their souls rose in their mouths
To shouts almost, they were so implicated.

Go--don't--why--oh why--I always said--
You never did--not possible--impossible--
Possible--oh Clay--never--oh Clay--
He could ride them, that boy.

So I read the *S.F. Chronicle* as if I were reading.
And by and by he got up and came over and took it away.
And said, don't you care?
And I said, yes I do. But I did not get into the argument.

CITY

What is my home, what is my city and home,
My avenue of palms, where the traffic ever
Rides and rides,
My Telegraph Avenue where the message filters,
My Shattuck Square of stores?

You are my home, you are my city lights
In which the morning sun entangles when it comes
Over our shoulder like an Easter.
You are my western loss
That brings the city back into its shine.

And I am my home, I am my country town
Through which the highway roars that 101
Leads on its way.
I am the town that to your highway turns
And goes along with it a little while.

NATURAL WORLD

From our view there is evil in the natural world.
Storms are unkind, lavas burn our shores,
Waves toss and turn us, winds also.
From the world we are hard put to it to preserve ourselves.

Yet there is good in it, when the day dawns
Kindly on our spirits, or the winter weather
Abates, and the quiet night
Looms. And these are our conditions.

Now the question is: Fire? Fruit from the tree? In these futures
Burrows the question of diverse answers
Where the storm says no, and we answer yes to it;
The waves yes, and we reply against it.

In this diversity do we oppose,
Or do we further by a further insight,
Or share another source within
The storm cloud and wave?

Then in and out, high and low fall together
In deep and shallow, and the soul
Ruffles its surfaces. Yet by legend
The storm still blows from the left hand, and thunder from heaven.

NUMEROLOGY

Plurality, my element by which I feed
And which I dread,
A hundred thousand in which I
Am magnified

To live and breathe, I avoid.
And I think on one,
Other and never whole
But alien.

Think dream gasp toward a two
To simplify
And ease the wealthy welter
Of plurality.

While couple and couple my friends gasp and dream
Out of the dual in which they are hid
Toward an immensity
They must afford.

KITCHEN

What will allow
The sun and moon
To rest in the square kitchenette without quitting,
Or the Bible
To dictate to the cookbook?

What will permit
Egregious contemplation

To affront utensils of a common day
And furnish
Completed recipes?

Oh how in Mesopotamia
These pots and pans
Would rattle and clink in its rich wilderness
And lose themselves.
Would they reclaim their domesticity?

Vessels of self
Swept with the sun and moonlight can contain
Cosmos and more,
A bounteous prophet's sky
Within a recipe.

CLOUD

Strontium 90 is slowly falling out
From the great heights of the stratosphere.
It settles
On leaves, on housetops, on ourselves
When we stand out under the open sky.
It settles down

In the grass which cows mull into their milk,
Which children gulp into their skeletons.
How much of the stuff is now in the skies?
A good deal is up there.
It drifts and settles out,
Half of it in about twenty-four years.

In my wristbone turns up Strontium 90 a-crumble
In your set jaw, its lag.
The mortal dust we have knelt in the dust to
Rises at the horizon, so that we move
Drawing out of the mire and blowing
Clouds of the mire ahead of us as we go.

PAINT

When the old man died, the folks got the old lady
To go to her sister's in Mendocino for a short stay.
And when she walked out of her house to Al's Chevy
It looked as if she were walking from one grave to another.

Then Marguerite her daughter and Marguerite's husband
Pitched in for the weekend and fixed the place over,
Waxed up the floors, washed windows, hung fresh curtains,
Even repainted the old lady's bedroom.

It always had been white, an off-white; now they went down
and bought
One of the new greens, called avocado. Something different.
When the old lady got back, about a day early,
They hadn't got the furniture in place, but she could get the effect.

She was nowhere near so pleased as they had hoped.
Tired from the trip and all, she looked lost in the avocado,
But her daughter said, Mama cheer up, it will certainly fade some.
So she did.

from

Local Measures

1946

SO GRAVEN

Simplicity so graven hurts the sense.
The monumental and the simple break
And the great tablets shatter down in deed.

Every year the quick particular jig
Of unresolved event moves in the mind,
And there's the trick simplicity has to win.

CONTAINED

The beautiful intense light of intense morning
Allows the fullest speculation toward the day,
The reach of every hand and hope outward
To come what may.

The noon the afternoon the night and after
Are all implied in the free life of green,
And morning's self-contained. But looks to windward
For more to be seen.

Neither events complete nor sun's attainment
Are enough thought for the green to gather in.
It's the pure black hope of morning so greens it,
The notion of again.

BLOOM

The steamfitter comes home in a pink cloud plainly
Keeps his helmet clapped on his head vainly,
It's a new day, season, and 7 A.M. only.

The quinces ripen in their most lurid blossoms,
They thicken on every side the streetcar pathways,
The dog-tired steamfitter gets home between them.

One plush of quince at his own door he will doff to,
Take in the dawn his hard steel helmet off to,
But bush will not bend or petal blow, it's so early.

HOUSEWIFE

Occasional mornings when an early fog
Not yet dispersed stands in every yard
And drips and undiscloses, she is severely
Put to the task of herself.

Usually here we have view-window dawns,
The whole East Bay at least some spaces into the room,
Puffing the curtains, and then she is out
In the submetropolitan stir.

But when the fog at the glass pauses and closes
She is put to ponder
A lifeline, how it chooses to run obscurely
In her hand, before her.

IN AIR

What's in the air is won, the air over,
The veriest pebble and blade, the air over,
Veriest peak and plane, air over
Hope and hope.

What's in every listener's head, said or not,
Air resting said in every listener's head,
Is hoped and won.

What's hoped is breathed and blown over every town
And so banked and reeled over every field
And so borne aware
In every grain of air.

Puffs in the nebulae and spins and spreads
In the starheads,
The hope and care won in our very air.

GYPSY

The entire country is overrun with private property, the gypsy
king said.

I don't know if this is true,
I believe in the gypsy kingship though.

The lost tribes of my own nation
Rove and rove.
In red and yellow rough and silent move.

I believe
The majesty pot mending, coppersmith
On the hundred highways, nothing to do with.

And black eyes, black I never saw,
Searching out the pocket lines of cloth,
The face lines and the furrows of belief.

It's a curious fact, Stephan, King, if you are made to doubt
Aegyptian vision on the Jersey shore.
Property's private as ever, ever.

OPAL

The steamfitter had no notion of buying an opal,
But a stone comes sudden in its meaning often.

He looked for a new watch, that part of his life, there was none,
He had to furnish his own time sense.

But this opal. Fire of time that burned in the antique reaches,
Roman omen, power of the sooth.

How comes so much actual straight evil into an opal?
Fix on a streak of bad luck, it goes out.

How comes so much red, then green, into an opal?
There aren't those colors in a glass of milk.

His wife didn't want the jewel but he bought it
And took that burden on, which fate forbore.

FRIEND

As I was going past Capstan's Well
I met a man in a woolen reefer,

A friend of my friend's.
What was his disposition?

He was bald as a bat,
Blind as an egg,
Bent as a lion, bold as a bird.
A singular complex of idiosyncratic qualities.

Then let me explain, said the man in the reefer,
I too am a friend of a friend and a dream of a dreamer,
A classical character often.
And often beloved.

MAN OF LETTERS

He had a reading eye which used to find
Jacks-in-the-box in the paragraph, jacks to open,
And nobody ever drew to any better.

What he could see in Hawley-Smoot or the races,
Kayak II's health for example, always had spring to it,
Jumped with a very grace from where in print it lay.

Take a long waste area of four hundred square pages with him,
And probably find before one hundred fifty
A bubbling spring, a joyful cap and bells, out at you.

O words so kind and human kind to take
That fortune from his eye, or give it to him,
Sprouts in the sentence, royals in the voice.

FORECAST

All our stones like as much sun as possible.
Along their joints run both solar access and decline
In equal splendor, like a mica chipping
At every beat, being sun responsible.

How much sun then do you think is due them?
Or should say, how much sun do you think they are apt to have?
It has misted at their roots for some days now,
The gray glamour addressing itself to them.

I should think possible that it go on misting likewise
A good way into next year, or time as they have it,
A regular cool season every day for our stones.
Not a streak that low of any sun or longed surprise.

EFFORT FOR DISTRACTION

for Henry Adams

Effort for distraction grew
Ferocious, grew
Ferocious and paced, that was its exercise.

Effort for distraction strained,
Legged in the hour-like single stretch
Its heels and sight to feel, so slit its eyes.

Effort without effort or with
Greatest possible effort always centered
Back in the concentrated trough where lies

The magnet to the filings,
The saw tooth to the tongue,
The turn of life to a returning life.

By all the traction of mind and spin of spirit
Having gained grasp gasped to bear it,
Having got ground groaned, furious title holder.

Paced and cried, so sore for a different direction, grew
Ferocious, grew
Unkind to strength that gave it strength to grow.

DENIAL

Events like the weeping of the girl in the classroom
Bring to the demands of objects
Denial pure and simple.

Denies the sun, desk, hand, head of the girl,
Denies the book, letter, document,
Denies the ether of the natural will,

Any event like the crying of girl
In the chair in the sun
In the passion of denial.

HERO

I liked the small pale man who leaned, I liked the twenty-
Five-year-old explorer at the pole of age,
The wan producer who knew his own desire.

I heard the quiet hero in the story relate
His long intention, and no more that day,
And that was crisis in its merest mention.

This one unshouting unleading and unpleading
In a creased still assurance tentative,
Waiting a magnitude to confirm and tally.

The ghost I liked, the young pale pole beater
Back with content and conscience, being ready
For a self-portrait in the face of State.

SPEAKER

My talking heart talked less of what it knew
Than what it saw.
Look, look, said it.
An index to the sights.

Spoke less it saw than what it wished it saw.
See, see, said it.
An index to the heart
And not the countryside.

My talking heart, will it then take the task
From look and look
To say, I wish and want
And say, I know?

MERCHANT MARINE

Where is the world? Not about.
The world is in the heart
And the heart is clogged in the sea-lanes out of port.

Not in the work or the west,
Not in the will or the wriest
Task is the world. It is all seaward.

Chart is the world, a sheet
In the hand and a paper page,
A rendable tissue of sea-lanes, there is the heart.

TOURISTS

Genealogists, geologists, and experts in falconry
Walked over the green and stony island and approved it,
Looked in the face its people and passed by them
As a rock unprocessed.

Jotted down traces of races, croppings, and the brooded bird,
The eyries of a scandic shift to believe,
But more closely what to name ancestral and to make
What plunge in the feathered spot.

Lifted on highways and at club festivals,
The host genealogists, geologists, and falconers making them
welcome,
Eyes to the host eyes, and pressed past them
To the height where the hood be lifted for work.

PLAYERS

Into the spacious bay the sun of afternoon
Shone,
And there two people, a man with a beard and a woman without,
were playing
At cards alone.

Lake traffic, line traffic, pine, plain traffic all around them
Presided,

Roared but soft, rushed but not
Into the window many-sided,

Looking for a game to play, a war to win, some sort of magnificent
  errand
To be done;
While the spadebeard took easily a trick
Already a century won.

DOLOR

When swimming and croquet are in full sway, dolor
Asserts itself, rocks on the porches its own whited color.

Dolor dismayed with one life after another
Tells its tally, but never tells enough.

Never gets the last iota pat, never gets
Veronica buried, thought of her too late.

Extend, dolor, extend, assert, and let
No one walk to the post office in the middle of this.

Maintain on one sun porch, in one mild
Summer, one dismay unreconciled.

THE THOROUGHGOING

He killed and kept.
He doused the capital city in kerosene,
He chopped the maples up for firewood
And then it was the city they kept warm.
All winter warmed preserved and kept
For him.

He told the city fathers Die, and they
Died with unwillingness and shock and met again
Next weekday morning for the usual course
Of minor and perhaps a major bill.
All morning voted and vetoed the village ways and means
For him.

He had his uncle understand the old was dead,
Laid down the old man's bay in earth for a leaner muscle,
And grayly from the grave came home to find
The glitter of watch chain crossed his uncle's dinner.
Saved for him. The heirloom worn aloft and soft and now and still
Saved for him.

FUNERAL

They may go to the beach straight from the funeral,
You may not be able to reach them by any call,
They may not go home at all.

They may run in the sand in the stickers and the swell,
Their thought of the dead again and again more pale,
Putting him farther in town where you will call.

Out from themselves in the spray they may go away
And pay no mind to what you want to say,
And attend in the end the longer limp laming and lingering
  funeral.

THE SYMPATHIZERS

To this man, to his boned shoulders
Came the descent of pain.
All kinds,
Cruel, blind, dear, horrid, hallowed,
Rained, again, again.

To this small white blind boned face,
Wherever it was,
Descended
The blows of pain, it took as it were blinded,
As it were made for this.

We were there. We uneasy
Did not know if it were.
Knew neither
The reason nor the man nor whether
To share, or to beware.

LOSER

A gracious number of dark-witted thieves
Stole all I had, in a pack as thick as that.
I was so disappointed I rocked as I sat.

I chewed on a straw hoping it would get sweeter.
It got drier and drier
And gradually caught on fire.

I spat it out, nothing left to chew,
I looked up the street and I looked down,
I saw that everything was really gone.

The people who got the goods enjoyed them I guess
For they never brought them back fourfold in a dray
As I expected them to until this day.

PHOTOGRAPHER

The man to be photographed was a student of mankind
In sets, by which it lasted long.
And he read in a walnut room
Filled with the shadows of his projected thought.

One ship was stalled in oil, one carpet
Thread at his foot.
There was one vase gleamed in the forenoon
And another, after.

The photographer to get all this at all
Shoved back the blinds,
And set against the side of the portrayed studying forehead
A car-load sun.

CHARACTER

A movie light, I don't know what they call it, but it's white,
Cuts close the face,
Takes off the scar and grin
And makes it Michael, sir, and heaven-sent.

Light cuts so close, and slices down the character so fine,

Makes profile out
A mountain range serene
Against a sky and makes the twilight airs come down and purify.

If it is not the man you know but only soul
Cast on the screen
In cut from brow to chin,
Have patience, few but camera read him so, and camera's hounded
by the show.

PREDICTION

Ah face that has my heart in it
Corner for corner and mile for mile,
What will I do when in the instant coming
You look to smile?

All spires, acres, faces will be smiling
In just such sudden; there will be
All I ever knew, down to the last straw even,
Looking at me.

CONDUCT

How conduct in its pride
Maintains a place and sits
At the head of the table at the head of the hall
At the head of the hosts and guests.
Bring on the time.

Conduct, the nodding and laughing all are yours.
How gracefully and fine
The head turns on its stem
At the end of the table at the end of the house
And yours are all the becks and listening ears.

Bring on the several salads. See the crowd
Ready and reticent in its waiting sits
Leaving the whole thing up
To conduct in its garb
To do the anecdotal smiling, yes.

CIVIC PRIDE

Between two warehouses the inner city
Rose up and shone,
Marble and magnificent in moonlight.
Where is its mayor? It has none.

Council? None too. PTA,
All those glosses? None anywhere. We were dismayed
And surrendered that dream up to the warehouses, dumb,
And trod back the scurvy civic pavement whence we had come.

LUCIFER ALONE

One rat across the floor and quick to floor's a breeze,
But two a whisper of a human tongue.
One is a breath, two voice;
And one a dream, but more are dreamed too long.

Two are the portent which we may believe at length,
And two the tribe we recognize as true.
Two are the total, *they* saying and *they* saying,
So we must ponder what we are to do.

For every scuttle of motion in the corner of the eye
Some thought of thought is asked in us indeed,
But of two, more: there we have likeness moving,
And there knowledge therefore, and therefore creed.

WHAT FOLLOWED

In all happiness and peace of mind
The man spoke a villainy, he was sore at it
And would have it back but it was gone already,
Ducked in the pool of the past and there no diver,
It was done for and he with it, he said.

But the very villainy got up of itself,
It was so light it ran, and he after it,
Asking everybody as he ran where it went to,
All had seen it and spoke of it to him,
They knew him by it.

When one summer eve in another county
He met up with the villainy at a concert,
Asked how it did, and said Here am I,
My whole life and place of life changed by chasing you,
He found he held its leash, it was his seeing eye
Purchased and instructed.

ALL HALLOW

The lady in the unbecoming bonnet
Let down her weeping hair.
She saw the broomstick and the witch upon it
Riding there.

The wind was full of bottles and the air
Aggressive as a shell.
The lady watched about her everywhere
The sallyings of hell.

The little boys stopped ringing at the bell
As she came homeward sadly. They had her cat
Spitting and mewing, a black one: Lady,
Whose cat is that?

CONFIDENCE

Thank you for your kind attention.
    How the ear can rest upon the heart.
    The long bolster of a life story
    Fresh at the ear and in every mention
    Full of comfort.

Rest and attend again, for if more beating
Trembles in the heart to attend
It will be an undertale and differing story,
The second speech, a plea, and the more fleeting,
Told to the friend.

MIDWEEK

Plentiful people went to the Cadillac drawing,
My ticket was number nine seven two seven one,
And my friend's ticket was number nine seven two seven two,
Certainly a lucky number and easy to remember.
I thought of it all through the film, and I like Greer Garson.

O heaven when the lights went up, the table trundled in,
The number called didn't even begin with a nine.
There wasn't even that much respite of hope after the happy
ending.
That is the kind of change the brave buckle
Time and again to.

All those people heart-rent and rustling,
I wished the upper lights would not look down so,
The curtain not so aquamarine, the manager not in tuxedo,
Me not so pale. I wished the second feature
Dark and dreadful.

REDEMPTION

The extra-well-made movie ups and outs
In a soft snow falling, that's the extra.
Whatever sin of shock or corn was there
The snow redeems.

Or doves redeem, in a high flight flying,
The nineteenth-century bird of blessing and belief.
There goes the soul, says Warners, up
Up into the air.

But, Brothers, see it fail. The birds fly,
Clouds fail in an unwilling flare.

Affairs now fostered are not fostered by
Any resolving sky.

OUTSIDE

Ever saw sidewalk uninterpreted?
This is one.
The Rialto sidewalk with environs
Makes no sense.

What does it give sea legs after a sea picture?
Gum papers.
What does it give spurs after range riding?
A slippery basement tilt.

Any other sidewalk fits the foot,
Takes in and out of doors and miles away
Any number of acknowledging steps,
You lead, I follow,

I take you up on that.
But this cementy floor makes no legitimate offer.
It extends for the night-flight survivors
To alight, not awake, but walk over.

ACT V

Pit, balcony, plush black,
Mind and the resource of mind black,
The buried caved-in coal mine of spirits
Arm to arm, black to black,
Had dawn break from the wings.

Alpine or Zebraian dawn started up,
Flitted on the convinced pillar and prop,
Purely promised in the dawn's darkest,
And then grew and again grew
In the impatient impossible increase of the new.

When it reached the windows it slanted in,
And at the arm-to-arm unheard remembrances it slanted in,

One after one, the individual dawn,
Wing-born, in all that blackness hard to bear
Upon the midnight of a different day.

DANCER

The foot and knee of the dancer
Must learn the room he is in.
Must seek in the room of the dancer
Its special pleasure.

Whether of draw and rise
Whether of cramp and fawn
Whether of extensive and ambling leisure,
The identifiable measure.

The room of the dancer changes,
The way-stations of his ways
Collapse from hall ranges
To tiled bays

And back expand, flicker.
The toe's to tell
To the doubting heart of the dancer
If these mean well.

To tell to the cord of the dancer
What footing and follow is
On every fleeting platform,
And what platform his.

THE DISTURBED

They drummed salvation in the darker districts
And a man cried Save me.
They closed the circle up, he was not a sober sinner.

He pushed at the corner crowd and came at them.
Save me.
They closed the placards round that said Repent.

Easy easy there, the tall young preacher murmured.
Save me.
See my scars, I repent, replied the desperate sinner.

Pull up my shirt and see the scars on my stomach.
Save me.
They are my sins, count them, the sinner cried.

Then to the increased crowd the three soft
Sopranos started singing Judgment,
Jubilee for the unsaved and the unsober.

SUBDIVISION

Three dogs bark at the street end, hear, this
Is a wild region, animals talk in audible sound,
What if one called it baying, then for 1104
Or 1107A or 1126½
Death were inevitably taking up the ground.

But ground here? ground with its growl and limitation
Not here at avenue. The poorest is paved and scaped.
And lift eyes, one will see the fuel of perpetual dawn
Over 1100 block as over
The civil civic center where it is shaped.

Dog again, it is disturbed. In this briefest meantime
Municipal hum has taken itself close in
And does not as on milder nights accompany
To the 1100 bed and board
The soft-soled progress of the citizen.

Dog answers and agrees; o pioneer,
Five blocks to windward hear the click of rails
Bearing their car away, hear faulting up
Near to 1100 block and nearer
The hoary quarries and the scrub of hills.

ILLUMINATION

The light burns in the foliage, but the bushes
Will not burn.

The light flares and fades but the bushes in the dark
Assume no single spark.

The willows in the water drink and survive,
Greening the channel water.
The black world moist and green
Where the light burns to be seen.

The incendiary mind of light pours its array
Leaf over leaf the light.
The full foliage thickened, the green bough bloomed
Will not be consumed.

NONE

A nothing out of which to create a new
Was never nothing enough for a new, never
Empty lost lone nought enough
To come clean new in any morning light.

Always in that limbo wide as it was,
Deep, down, as it was, somebody lay
Qualifying any possible creation.
Toppled in that void tossed there, and woke.

from

Prefabrications

1955

BOMBAY

If I woke in Bombay it would be possible
The rooftops would confuse me, and the dying men,
Accustomed as I am to the skyline of the living
And the jerrybuildings of tomorrow's life.

But it is not possible that when in confusion
I fled in the street, frantic for familiar sight,
I should not see in some face there
Your look as Indian as dense with life.

SON

Men have their alien sons and love them,
The dear fist clenched in theirs,
The foreign taste fed at their table,
The wayward walking in their name.
They love their handsome son.

But they hate the foreign, though an open
Five-fingered hand like theirs,
The gall taste deep as another nation,
The ugly accent in an alien name.
Hate all but him, dear father, and dear son.

SIEGE

The courtyards of the inner heart go round
And round, so sure are they
Where they will end; the brick
Convolutions enter and extend
The individual life, and come to end.

Beyond, the plains of the universe compass hope
So thin so fast
A television cannot trace what spins
Political or polar in the shape
Of one quick trip.

Between, in middle distance where the seasons
In plenitude emerge,
Figures move together on the open
Course, out of the beleaguered heart,
Out of the universal siege.

HOLIDAY

Returning from the north, I saw the sun returning
In the same car.
Back to our indigent county we retreated
From the summer war.

All us vacationers, dead, alive, burnt,
Said as we rode
That to live up to the Fourth of July, Christmas
Would have to be pretty good.

And we rode in the memory
Of the rockets' red glare
Blazing and disintegrating to our vision
In the soft summer air.

But the sun was recollecting in its wide glance,
Passive and regional,
Necessities of a colder danger, with the chance
Of a warmer festival.

THE DAY THE WINDS

The day the winds went underground I gasped for breath,
Did not you?—oxygen gone from the chest wall,
Nostrils pinched in the scant weather, strictest
Sort of equilibrium at street corners.

It was a pity. Who could walk in the hills now
Or run for a train? The water in a storm
Ran down the sides of buildings and the bark of trees
Straight down, like tears.

In the first days it was not so desperate;
I remember, though short of breath,

Thinking with relief in the dense quiet,
Fall will be quiet.

But more and more as the streets clogged with traffic
And the smog of the city's production lay on its eyes,
One could notice persons burrowing, hearts hammering,
Toward the risks of the wind.

EVANGEL

What happens when the evangelist of truth
Waves his arms, shakes his fist once?
Does the truth stand by him?

What happens when the donkey of radiation
Brays in his corral?
Is it true?

What happens when in electric fields of low intensity but immense
extent
Perturbations are set up in a westerly current?
Cyclones move faster when they are young?

Evangelist! Westward the course of empire takes its way
And every traveler asks what way is west,
What west is true.

SALE

Went into a shoestore to buy a pair of shoes,
There was a shoe salesman humming the blues
Under his breath; over his breath
Floated a peppermint lifesaver, a little wreath.

I said please I need a triple-A,
And without stopping humming or swallowing his lifesaver away
He gave one glance from toe to toe
And plucked from the mezzanine the very shoe.

Skill of the blessed, that at their command
Blue and breathless comes to hand
To send, from whatever preoccupation, feet
Implacably shod into the perfect street.

FIND

Diligent in the burnt fields above the sea
The boy searches for what, sticks,
Cans; he walks like a rider
The rough and stumpy ground.

And finds all morning while the sun
Travels to crest, a blooming fullness of day,
Just one ant-paste spike, rusted.
Says the boy with relish, *Poison.*

Often at night his fears have told him these
Dooms to find in the hills, and his heart lightens
To find them there in fact, black as intended,
But small enough.

SUMMER

When I came to show you my summer cottage
By the resounding sea,
We found a housing project building around it,
Two stories being painted green row after row
So we were set in an alley.

But there is the sea I said, off the far corner
Through that vacant land;
And there the pile of prefabricating panels
And the cement blocks swiftly
Rose in the sand.

So darkened the sunlit alley.
Ovid, Arthur, oh Orion I said, run,
Take Rags with you, send me back
News of the sea.
So they did, vanishing away off and shouting.

RAIN

When I came to the porch
The faces that I met
Were family faces
Sheltering out of the wet.

When I came to the door
The presidential race
Was being run off
Over the mantelpiece.

When I came to the stair
The word of the Lord
Met me, and it was not
A welcoming word.

But all through the mansion
Of retired men
Murmured the louder and the louder insurrection
Of the louder and the louder rain.

RIOT

What strength give to riot that it can subside?
O hungry riot, here and here is food,
Eat and rest.
Comfort the little riot. Love is best.

But the big little roarer leaps from the breast,
Hungry, angry, and for no good.
And what then
Cries mother, cries uncle, to the rioting man?

BELIEF

Mother said to call her if the H-bomb exploded
And I said I would, and it about did
When Louis my brother robbed a service station
And lay cursing on the oily cement in handcuffs.

But by that time it was too late to tell Mother,
She was too sick to worry the life out of her
Over *why why*. Causation is sequence
And everything is one thing after another.

Besides, my other brother, Eddie, had got to be President,
And you can't ask too much of one family.
The chances were as good for a good future
As bad for a bad one.

Therefore it was surprising that, as we kept the newspapers from
  Mother,
She died feeling responsible for a disaster unverified,
Murmuring, in her sleep as it seemed, the ancient slogan
Noblesse oblige.

BARGE

Everywhere the lights of the settlements
Are steadfast in their place, the streets of Tiburon
Straight up the hill, and bridges
Horizontal at the shortest distance.

On the near shore the Reynolds' radio burns
Red under its lamp, and our little blazes
Flickering and wavering, turn steady
Finally, in the stiff breeze.

Then from the pier pulls out into the tide
Silently a barge, bearing its lights
Three singly, across the neighborly water,
Moving like conscience toward the longest distance.

TWO KINDS OF TROUBLE

for Michelangelo

1
Ruin of David directly offers
Determination out of two thousand years
Which meager and young rose from its lesson

And took its sling in hand,
Head saying what hand has crumbled away.

Ruin of Adam, in his fibers the plaintive
Contortion of desire to live forever
Lives in a second vision forever,
Trunk at the twist of aspiration
Learned of a natural content, with hardship.

Ruin of Evening, robes heavier
On the spirit than dark, the wealth of abendland
Weighting the arms and eyelids, over the breast
Brood of somnolent passion, of long
Dreaming to come.

Ruin of Zeus and of Pope Julius,
Hard men together in sinew of authorship,
Jaws at the clench, giants of David
Breathe their curly beards and blue beards
On the Atlantic rime, over to us.

Ruinless. To us, ruinless. Their gaze westward
Casts on fields of lettuce and rye
Message of a dimension for us,
Length of the time of ruin in the world,
Breadth of the shoulders of its magnitude.

2
When God said let there be light
The Darkness said let there be light
In the dark irony of his being.
His chill assurance plucked the nursing sun
Daily from its place in heaven.

The suave embittered Dark
Sworn to his resurgence
Sat easily under the palm of the Lord
Like a lord,
His fillet Roman.

How can the supple day
Move from this desperate work
Heaving and sweating in the whirlwind,
Mild as a morning air
Into the morning?

It is one thing to see
Once the snake-ridden tree of Eden,
And another ever to pursue the shoulders bent
From Eden's discontent
Into the fortunate wilderness of stone.

Adam is unruly
In Noah and again
In David, in Zachariah and again in Jacob,
Looks God in the eye his frown and says
Let there be light, in irony of being.

3
I heard how Zachariah read out of his book
Warnings,
Warnings heavy and heavy-lidded
While two boys glanced over his shoulder
All they could never want to learn.

And how Jeremiah put down the book,
Put down the robe of authorship,
Learned in his beard
The brunt of suspicious answers,
A heavy lesson.

Most gently I heard Daniel, when the breeze from the sea
Blowing his hair
Made him look away
To where in the locks of his heart the dark and the morning
Were saying there was light.

It was over the river, up from the channels of death
The caverns and waters
Bonds of bone
Into an arc as of morning
The lightest body rose.

To which now the Popes, youths, and cherubs,
Eyeing askance the dark lip of Adam,
Hearing askance the sun cry at even,
High at heaven,
Answer in irony.

4
About the mission of Rio Carmelo,
About the mission of San Juan Bautista, San Miguel,
Santa Barbara, better preserved,

Autumn crickets sing in the shrubbery
And wild grasses. At Carmelo
The river runs into the thickening sea.

From San Juan to Carmel and then down
Over the ridges the chaparral burns the sun away,
The great oven of air ladling herbs
To grill of ground, as ripe a medicine
As ever breathed corpse its new message,
Earth will consume and save.

I remember
How out of Florence the white roads ran
Precisely in their way
Along the poplar run.

The towered hills
In terraces as sharp
As statues in the noon's
Untoward light.

With marble
To the foot as to the hand,
The wealthy processes
Of civic state.

Vertical and discrete
All alleys, somber
All plaza squares
Like jewels of thumb.

Down which,
Fleeing in Chirican sequences,
Our author ran
In the cool of night

To Rome
And back again. To Rome
And back again, the agile
Paces of flight.

No more to flee
Florence than the board
On which he drew the squares
In black and white.

5

Maybe Sacramento is our town
Florence reminds you of.
A capitol base.
An oasis in the desert plain,
Pearl vanilla slums this side the tracks
And domes the other.

What is wonderful here is the air-conditioning.
While the sycamores
Draggle second-story verandas
In the canyon blast, as if an eyelid closed
Against a noon escape,
Here all the while the air-conditioning

Cools triplicates, controls
Every attic souvenir, cards
Every resentment which a grandfather spent
On down to a grandson since the Civil War
And quickly
Guides it through committee.

Well then, what of heritage we have
Goes well here in bar and grill
After the aspect of a lottery
Or confederacy,
Southern or south Chinese or south State Street
To which one fled away.

To Rome or Florence
Where he took up the marble
And made the marble face
In which there lived
Then on, the master of Medician trouble
Into good times and bad.

There lived on, in the stone of the forest
Everything he fled,
The crime in the face of the master of trouble,
The wrong he did,
The corruption he dreamed,
His jaw locked against a word of good.

And by the massive monument
Of self condemned
Self perpetrated and self fled to Sacramento

Came into his ugly ownership to live
To time forever
Even to California.

6
Now what I fear for our golden arroyos,
Their golden leaves and stones,
When the mesquite burns in the dusk and the small shadows
Of our fleeing sculptor fall on the roads, is

That he see no face of evil for his conscience
To clarify. That he see no hawk-nose
Greed sharp and angular in our capitol
Nor no sneer sinister nor scowl.

And again no bully chin bare in our capitol,
Barrel-jawed in our anterooms, no jut force,
Nor sleek sinews if you will, wry in the wisdom of
Persuasion drawn lithe at lip and tongue.

Nor cruel hollow eye nor empty ear
Nor bleak brow nor cheek broken and hurt
Nor twisted aspect at the temples' drill
Of rough unlatitude.

Not any ugly passionate powerful visage
Of man or stone to carve in anger
And to make our ruin,
But all air-conditioned.

Rather, I fear the photos of men of distinction
Fluttering in the low washes of the West
In the mesquite underbrush will breathe and tell
What we may know of life.

Smooth faces, smooth smooth faces
Good mood good personality faces
Smiling easy eager
Tender coy.

Round bland planned personality faces
Church porch porch faces
Blind rind never mind faces
Honest jolly.

Pink think mink portraits
Of bland good blind men of distinction

Presidents and pards, patriots
And paternosters, and their smooth faces.

Rather I hope the hard and difficult choice
That takes the stone and carves it to our hand
The deepest lines of human character
That wrong in the teeth of time asserts itself, its rough anxiety.

7

Down the alleys and arroyos drift
Pages from the nameless magazines
Of our life, sift the bushes
In the heavy sand.

At the arches of the old adobes,
At the doorways of the ranchos grandes,
Slip the pictures of our easy strangers
In their two-tone spreads.

And a good man is hard to find,
Whether from home or from his author's mind,
Whether from stone or from the complex mesh
Of Zeus in Adam's flesh.

From good and wrong
And irony of spirit,
Big enough for ruin
Should he choose.

RIDE

It's not my world, I grant, but I made it.
It's not my ranch, lean oak, buzzard crow,
Not my fryers, mixmaster, well-garden.
And now it's down the road and I made it.

It's not your rackety car but you drive it.
It's not your four-door, top-speed, white-wall tires,
Not our state, not even, I guess, our nation,
But now it's down the road, and we're in it.

THE HALT

The halt looks into the eyes of the halt and looks away.
No response there that he can see
To receive amply or repay.

But the halt will lead the blind; indeed,
Note how the generous stick gestures to precede
The blind, blundering in his black, black, black need.

DIALECTIC

Well, yes, you are as angry as we feared.
But fearful fighter, why? this anger
  blows up in your atmosphere
  like a magic storm
  brewed by vendors.

And when we say all's fair here, fair enough,
Bite to the quick that slight gentility
And blast the battered hob.
  It's a black
  enemy, by dialectic.

What would we do without hate? it makes ones two,
Wholes half, hearts hack, and a hullabaloo party
  after every meeting.
  It does transcend a duller habit
  and synthesizes from defeat, defeat.

REASON

Said, Pull her up a bit will you, Mac, I want to unload there.
Said, Pull her up my rear end, first come first serve.
Said, Give her the gun, Bud, he needs a taste of his own bumper.
Then the usher came out and got into the act:

Said, Pull her up, pull her up a bit, we need this space, sir.
Said, For God's sake, is this still a free country or what?
You go back and take care of Gary Cooper's horse
And leave me handle my own car.

Saw them unloading the lame old lady,
Ducked out under the wheel and gave her an elbow,
Said, All you needed to do was just explain;
Reason, Reason is my middle name.

AGGRESSOR

Restless animosity can sharpen its saber
On broadloom. I fear that rich flooring.
Or it can take fire from a Venetian screen.
I fear those paper shades.

The aggressions of the still room never
Let be the animus till it defends them,
Strikes and defends them, and the petty
Passerby is done to death. I fear him.

EXTENSION

The longer diameters
Lying in the plane of the Milky Way
Assert their strength.
Which of us could lie to such a length?

Clearest extension
From this point to that point far and away
Establishes the endurance
We are come to prove.

BIBLIOGRAPHER

Bad quartos were my first love.
Ever since,
I have worked in the particular possession
Of their providence.

Though increasingly wild the world
And as death corrupt,

My first love brings me succor
As I learn its script.

So that, in my presence,
Rank and complete
Spoil and error
Are not really dissolute.

I will take them up
And gently gent-
Ly love them, tell them
What they have probably meant.

HEADLESS

The man with no ears
Overhears
People talking in the park and lobby.
He is upset,
Their private ramblings concern him,
Do not let him forget
He has no ears.

What about the whole head then—
Placed either side,
Those fine organs of discrimination
Clean to the breeze—
Is it not possible such a head will hear
Just that which is spoken
And no more?

Rather, by often chance,
The delicate receivers
Bring to the brain such overtones of remorse
The whole head must operate like a blind man
Deaf and mute
Decline
To all or nothing.

And the choice
Nagging past bell to book or bark to voice
Past no to yes
Past yes to irony

Holds him the head up till its listening spirit
Wishes the hearing
Headless of itself.

EDUCATION

I would sit in the window's ledge
At Los Angeles High School
To watch the pecking sparrows
To hear the bickering girls
Their warm and lively life.

The sun that shone thereon
Would draw to warmest life
The coldest bone and silent
To ruffle in its dust
Bicker its edge of sun.

Now what shall I say of the cat
That sprang the pecking sparrows
What of the aunt that ate
The slightest bickering girls
What of the heart

Once warmed by delicate rays
Now sheltering all that sun
Till it would bless and blaze
A thousand windows in
A universe of schools?

STUDENT

Who is that student pale and importunate
Whom I have left with a heavy burden and forgotten all about?
Who wakes me as I fall asleep, asking
What I want done with the job now that the year's over.

And indeed I remember now he has been doing all my work,
Setting up the experiments, kidding the bystanders,
Puzzling the problems, and I have forgotten him
Till now too late, and must wait until morning.

Who is he? my thought which I deny until the dark,
Or one literal person I have now forgot
Who, early in the alphabet, recited
More than I could learn until tonight?

APARTMENT

Apartment hearts within their hearts so lie
Their hearts are all their own economy,
And trade too terrible, current too quick,
To tempt the resident to try his luck.

The resident indeed is filled with pride
He's so sufficient and unsatisfied,
And stays his quarrel by a long-term lease
And draws his walls within, and sues for peace.

HELDENLEBEN

Busy sickness, pay me attention, said a hero
Falling down, with his bland beak encored,
An accumulation of agues in his power
Ready to devour, should he give the word.

He hesitated, with concern for some care
And necessary solicitude if he succumbed,
Saw no signs of any anywhere,
But could not unflatten whence he had unclimbed.

So gave the nod to a most petty fever
To burn with its eyes closed on his tough
And frank forehead; it could not burn forever,
And expired finally, but it was enough.

GRANDFATHER

When I transact divorces of the mind,
And am hailed in abstraction tangled like a city,

Strong and devoted, as absorbed as that,
Suddenly I look up and see grandfather green.

Green sycamores, green leafage, shade and sky,
Green form and shape, in motion to my hand,
Every shape a gift and every
Burden a reminder.

And I think, Pater and my fine fathers,
Your rich prose taught and taught us at its knee,
And still thunders its cloud we argue under,
Yet now we argue barest daylight, in the expanse of green.

TEN DREAMERS IN A MOTEL

1
Some people said the cabin
Wouldn't hold us two,
Two hundred and forty pounds,
Two hundred and twenty-two.

But note wherever we moved
Back or face to face
Outside the windows flew
Hundreds of butterflies.

So that within our walls,
Walls that denied us well,
Glimmered the wing that tells
All things are possible.

To elephant and elephant
Stalking exact apart,
The centennial memory
Of a light heart.

2
At this dinner I was telling you about
Next door to this motel
Was your pal your host,
And me, and a mother, daughter
Come to greet you back, how they loved you.

She for the past as if a bowl of carnations
Sat with the chicken;

She for the chicken;
He for the silverware.

The lines of life which moved between you
Like toy tramcars
Were also like toy speedsters
Building up speed.
An electric party.

Except, between us, you
And me met to greet you back,
Was absence still.
A freedom free enough to kill.

3
One day we started out
To pick up driftwood. I was interested
In a housing project there, I had heard a lecture
Illuminating the beach like lightning.
It was my concern
To raise on the shingle rows of boards
On which the great foundations could be built.

Rather, I found the shanties were up already,
And indeed down already, every one
Empty to the tide as if just then
They had been lived in but would live no more.
I turned round.
If I had been looking south I looked north
East west I turned.

4
On which of the many hills
Of suburbs out beyond the State Fair on Saturday morning
Did we pasture our goats?
Up down over the Marguerite Street district
We saw the angel ladders behind before us
But not that field in which our thoughts were bound.

Conceive if you can the animal desolation
Which besieged us on all sides other districts than our own.
We were, myself and self, not enough to ensure
Any comfort of company, but one who will say
So it is, and not let me deny, say
Let us go back by the municipal railway.

5
Carombed out of town in a comedy-chase fashion,
Police oblique to our path, and statues
Wheeled over, through Harlem, and all more wasteful as we went,
And ended up at this tourist cabin,
Its outlook, so it was said, restful.

Went to the window,
Pushed aside the curtains and there saw
That countryside we longed for: rocks,
Steep slopes of rocks, rubble and rusk of rocks.
What is it? and you said, *moraine.*

6
When we came back all the underpasses were flooded,
Highway 40 blocked off
And six inches of water at the supermarket.
So it was necessary to go round by the byroads.

So it was that we came to our street from a different view,
Saw our neighborhood from aside and below,
Stacked up the hill our houses in their shrub,
Their windows empty as an evening sky.

And so it was we saw that they dwelt without us,
Endured merrily as bastions against our presence,
Persons of note and self in the rainy evening,
Lampless and starless.

7
I saw a field of folk in fit array,
A circus field, or fair,
A tumbler tin-twister and auto-court carnival
Brought for the day.

Among which I went, larking and singing,
Crowding and wandering, till
Where was I? everybody wandered
While I stood still, longing

To find myself out, there to find,
And in relief
I felt at my shoulder, straight beside me,
Father or friend.

But it was not, but a strange
Present person who stood,
To whom that field fair and carnival
And I, he said, belonged.

8
I went to consult a psychiatrist on this morning,
A nervous woman, whose curly-headed four-year-old child
Played in the room, sitting staunchly
On a great medical scales.

I defended myself thus. It looks as if
All this weariness came from too much work,
But rather I think it a problem of person,
Friend or foe, fortune of parent or pardon.

The nervous psychiatrist ran her hand through her hair
And glanced at her watch. Have you taken a trip lately,
It would do you good, and take your mother with you,
She needs it more than you do.

Then I laughed to hear my own prescription
Given to myself with such good humor
In the gray weariness. But then she said also,
Take with you also my curly-headed four-year-old child.

9
I said to my iron class, I am desperate, desperate,
You must learn and you will not.
Each by each I looked to into the light and said
You are fast in darkness.

Each to each I said I am desperate, desperate.
Then one rose from his seat and sat beside me,
Touching my hand and saying, out of his daylight,
Do not despair.

10
Midway stayed at a court between there and here
Where woodsmoke rose up straight into the sky,
Cabin by cabin the suppers cooking
Far as the eye could see, the courts unfolding
Durable darkness.

It was the tent and citadel of the many stars,
It was the rampart of the loud highway
And we slept there, waking

Into the thunder and silence of the unfolding
Durable journey.

THE PLASTIC GLASS

A saint I heard of saw the world
Suspended in a golden globe; so I saw
Shattuck Avenue and the Safeway Stores
In Herndon's globe of friendly credit.

And where the care moved on, there the whole trash
Flats of Berkeley floated in suspense,
Gold to the Gate and bellied to the redwood
Cottages.

And I would ask the saint at what expense
This incorporeal vision falls to the lay mind,
And search the breast
For revelations of unquietude.

But in this dear and christian world the blessing
Falls not from above; the grace
Goldens from everyman, his singular credit
In the beatitude of place.

STATUTE

The way I would look at the world, the houses
Take up half, the horizon
Moves straight across the view.
And the base half is houses, the roof lines of houses
Marking off the blue.

By what aerial license would it be possible
To promote any other line?
The piteous valley vista, or the terrible
Subordination
Seen by plane?

I would legislate against the Icarian downfall
As against the ascent of F6,
And take care

That the great legal skies of human vision
Observe their human shore.

MEETING

Once there lived on the east side of the city
One who wished to meet
One who lived on the west side of the city,
A thousand miles away.

A thousand years went by.

Then the one who lived on the east side of the city
Set out on the main street
And met the one who lived on the west side of the city
Coming that way.

A thousand years.

Miraculous life! that in its brief and mortal
Progress achieved this union of intents,
Inevitability sprung from the improbable,
Volition moving in the paths of chance.

PRIDE

My pride should effect your escape,
It carries every key.
Its own trusty, and a good chiseling trusty,
It can at its own price set everybody free.

And that is pride's advantage, that though it keep
Jailed itself at an interminable wall,
It recognizes the graces of the free
And can dispense freedom from its cell.

IDEA OF JOY

The idea of joy, abruptly,
Like the idea of day,

Came and clothed the body of the lady
In an array

As of field or fire
And she withheld
Any comment on this procedure
Until it was revealed

That garmented in this glory
And clothed in this joy
She was at a loss for words completely
And knew not how to say.

So that I write for her
With secretarial speed
What she would have faithfully
Conceived and said,

That it was not joy which dressed her
So sudden as the day,
So bright as the fire,
But the idea of joy.

BELL

Only the halting and waiting bell of the train
Now dallies from the depot valley
And drifts its clear impatience up the lane
Like a lesser trolley.

For we would wait, but it would not, and it shames us.

Its abrupt meditations swung and renewed
Like any cow's in the briary valley,
The lyrical crystal will not be withstood,
Echoing to its folly.

It reveals its folly as we do not, and it shames us.

The summer dusk to the midnight dusk will keep us
Face to face in the shadow our eyes darken,
Lingering yet in the phrase of another making,
With the air shaken

By the bell in its split to a shout and a shout and it shames us.

GRAHAM-PAIGE

Graham-Paige, a car I once rode in,
Carried me out of this world, and I was afraid of that.
Who wouldn't be? You wouldn't be, I see you
Driving across an equal abyss your heart.

At every crossroad
Pause the exporters of their worldly good,
Patient as passive,
As if they would untravel if they could.

And my antique memory
Sifts me the Graham as if
Every crossroad
Were a crossways cliff.

So that the power at your hand and foot defrayed
Is all my expectation and dismay.
And at every turn you save me.
You slow and save.

EYESIGHT

My adequate eye, to print, package, curb
Adequate, and to the natural scene,
Sees leaf by leaf but not
Your thought by thought.

My adequate eye, to your forehead and front
Adequate, and to your offered glance,
Sees beat by beat but not
Your leafy heart.

My eye, closed, dreaming, and inadequate eye,
Sees several selves all yours and graced in light,
But not your delicate grist
And adequate grain.

AUTUMNAL

We have lost so many leaves
  in loss, loss, loss
Out of the sky,
What shall we do for shelter to live by?

Not roof shelter, but leaf shelter,
  the tentative
Crosswise cover
Which a thousand light ideas give.

Retire under somebody's constructed rafters
  or be grieved that a truthful brain
Exists under a truthful sky
With no palaver between.

MATTER OF FACT

In the midmost and sensible real of the years of my life
Hallucination like a storm
Comes to its feet beside me,
Named by your name and calling me by mine.

So that lamp, storm, student, and friend
As it were love me,
And it is my luck
To love them dearly, as you demand.

They are sensible real as the life of my years
And I love them
As a matter of fact.
And I love you as a fiction of theirs.

HEIGHT

Shoulder to head is the height of my life to me.
My level eye
Looks to his rib as his long and level eye
Looks to the sky.

Shoulder to head is the height of my learning, there
Heart to ear
Lectures for me to listen, as his ear
Listens the sphere.

Shoulder to head is a height never to reach
By an equality of speech
But by my speechlessness which ever is
More patient though less possible than his.

RIDDLE

You are a riddle I would not unravel,
You are the riddle my life comprehends.
And who abstracts the marvel
Abstracts the story to its sorriest ends.

But not your riddle. It is patent,
Never more than it says, and since that is
Impossible, it is the marvel
Nobody, as I am nobody, believes.

HEIR

This gray board fence turns blue in the evening light
And the sycamores reign down upon it their diadems,
And blue and green batter in wood and stems
The stems of light
Their green and golden gems.

At once, out of a million years of energy,
All turn to flesh—board, gate, and branch—
With that quick sunset wrench
Which seems like chance,
Not in the fashioning of entropy.

If then the flesh is yours, as now it is,
I have lost yard, sunset, and all
Into a mild greeting, and I call
The sunset to your thought, to tell it is
Parent apparent to your rich apparel.

KIND

When I think of my kindness which is tentative and quiet
And of yours which is intense and free,
I am in elaboration of knowledge impatient
Of even the patientest immobility.

I think of my kind, which is the human fortune
To live in the world and make war among its friends,
And of my version, which is to be moderately peaceful,
And of your version; and must make amends

By my slow word to your wish which is mobile,
Active and moving in its generous sphere.
This is the natural and the supernatural
Of humankind of which I grow aware.

from

"Neighbors and Constellations"
(Poems 1930-1960)

1960

A FOREIGN COUNTRY (1950)

I

Outside this room—from where you sit on the floor you can see it,
From where you lean your head back in the chair you can see it,
Out the arches of the windows
In the slanting western sunlight at your fingers' tips—
Russia extends, another country.

These trees we see grow in Russian territory
Just beyond Magnitogorsk, in what they call
Suburban acres, they thrive there.
The sky, pale blue today as the faintest sort of idea,
Floats over us, thinking another language.

Figure the Northwest-echoing forest of fir and pine,
The snowcapped peaks of the Caucasus
More remote more near than the Sierra.
Eastward across the Caspian the parched expanses
Where nomads pitch their tents like Arabs in the sun.

In central Asia the minarets of Tamerlane,
In Siberia, Mongolian Buddhists,
In the black earth, wheat grain and rye; by the Black Sea
Fruit orchards, vine terraces, tea plantations.
Oil at Baku, gold at the river Lena.

This is the world of hell, as if you saw the sky darkening
Just outside, always at arm's reach.
What once below in brimstone burned and languished
Now takes the topography of an earthly land mass
Contiguous to ours.

We are beside ourselves, and hell beside us
Flares up its fear
Even to the enigma of the sky we share.
And every human circumstance we share in
Turns foreign to protect our hesitation.

II

Consider that instant of anger when to the blow
Of fist or word your blood rises
Like a tide into the brain of hate,
And opposition is like a wall intolerable to protest.

That instant occurs not to the pure spirit
Of Magna Carta, but at the Dnieperostroy,
Where a club-fisted cavalry rides like a wall of iron
Against its innocent and starving victims.

Pity for self in pure oppression wells
Against the eyelids of the angry sleeper
And wakes him to the jolt of frozen winter
With the hooves of those riders full in his face. Defend.
And the face of those riders Russian to the core.

Along the street of a small Moldavian village
Warm with sun in the late afternoon
Walks the Red Dean. All the children
Run out to meet him, tumbling in the dusty mud,
Crying in the still slanting air,
Running to kiss the cross he bears.
The pastoral condition. I detest it.
Terrible condescension and blind
Enthusiasm in the color of everyday
Burden my thought, whether I am the keeper
Or the flimsy kept, red-robed as gospel bearer
Or as tattered as
The scrawny children running to be blessed.
One alien midget face after another,
Black-eyed and foreign to my blue regard,
Looks to that cross as if it were not mine.

What about the unjust vote on the floor of the chamber?
It was manipulated by an inner caucus
Of the party, false as a wig.
Inner spies, over whom the truth cannot prevail.

I spoke ably to the proposition,
Pled for the sincerity of our principle, marshaled the possible points
Briefly and succinctly. Yet we were voted down.
The totalitarian picture is unalterable.

In the great place where the avenue
Comes into the market square
There a statue is builded
To a living god.
Who builds a living god, his beard preserved
In formaldehyde? It deifies myself.
I will not be responsible to keep the corpse alive,
I will not feed my faith into that beard

Under that glass.
Dissolve the Sunday corpse on Monday morning
And let the living children jump and jump,
Like fleas the living godkins
Without beard.

But say your concern is electrification, solely,
A large production platform like a plan
Rolled year to year, a forcing from the rock
The rush of waters at their giant source:
Would this not please you, the chain of dams reading
Down the Urals, over to Kazakhstan
To the tents of the Arabs? Power stations gleaming
And high wires like a blaze of concept
Above the chores of fact? I would like this better,
A turbine than a Safeway, Manager.
But still you pardon me. You know, better than I,
Within the grasp of continental power
How dangerously madmen preside. Roskolnikov for example
Murders up and down the attic stairs, you feel
You cannot trust this brooding Russian spirit
With any nice machinery of ours.
And indeed I see you are right.
As you spin the dials
And the lights come on again all over the world
There's something in your aspect darkens me,
The bitter mouth which Prince Alexei drew,
All that cavernous speculation
Which roars in the ears of the turbines like a wind
And hangs above the stars on Dienerplaza
A cloud of doom. O come
Out of that blackening power to the Safeway,
Store Manager, come home.

Moving a little eastward, our fear arrives
At Baku. Well-known Baku.
One of our trustees
Is thereto allied.
But what that gleaming substance
Would do to a less hardy pioneer
In the way of glossing
Is unthinkable.
Anyone who has ever stopped at a Standard station
Knows the cleaning-up oil has required

And so the oiled heart
In the glass house.

They say the streets of Izarka are built of well-polished timber
Like bridges over ground all year caked with ice,
The houses like chalets above these shallows,
And they grow cabbages in the nine-week sunlight
Between the night and night.
You could be alone.
Severe and honest as a single tree, a single stone.

Or, like Kurambek Alimozhanov, you might live more mildly
In a central district, a village in Kazakhstan,
And look from your cottage to the sun-flooded steppe
Flat as an eye can see, beginning the desert,
Noting, like a spar at sea horizon,
A commune tractor, driven by a Buryat Mongol woman you may
surmise;
She has her orders.

Free breath into the hearty lung,
Breath as the spacious plain,
Why drawn into the speculative lung
As if in pain?

The free grapes of freedom are sour.
No one knows how to cultivate them.
The tundras of the breast constrict,
The enviable spaces horrify us.

From continental doubt there echoes back
No intimate evil we would wish to claim,
But icy evil of vast enterprise
Would kill a man. And maybe has.

III

Troubled as was my sister by the crossing
Blocked by a red light, she stopped, waiting,
And mused at her own anger.
Red lights make me see red, she said,
And the more this one
When up and down the boulevard near and far
No car loomed in, the asphalt was all plain
Waiting to walk across.
An empty breeze ruffled the kelly jackets,
Everybody had to get somewhere there, and the world theirs,

Except the tyrant light which lit and lit
Against their coming and their going over.
And my sister said,
I know I would die
If many of these lights were set against me;
A light on buying butter, a gong on lipstick,
A clang on prayer, red on the morning paper,
A grievous grievous green on one-way progress.
My sister turned right around in the empty traffic
And stamped the continent of Asia under her heel.

My brother visited a Russian ship
When it came to the harbor.
He liked ships, and he liked to talk to people.
He came away scared.
It was a black rusted loaded and caked ship
Nowise shipshape.
Its captain a woman vast as a bale,
Its crew darkening from brow to brow
Cursing and turning away
From my brother the spy.

Glades of convenience
Where we rest and wither
Give us the sense of charm,
The early riots
Blending in together
Out of the way of harm.

Peaceful at age
Whatever age allows us,
We build the basement room
To keep in fashion
Lest the age surprise us
Before millennium.

Nook of Victoria,
In the Afric jungle
British or even here
Is what we dread to find not
In Siberia
For many another year.

The bloody children there
Nor rest nor settle
Nor speculate their strife

But spread the globe
In a perpetual battle
Against the glades of life
The golden in agreement
And midsummer
Glades of life.

What does Enemy mean?
Enemy?
Not who wants what you have,
He is an envious friend.
Not who has what you hate,
He is your fond acquaintance.
Not who needs what you need,
He is your fearful stranger.
But what you are,
Whose death will be your death,
Whose life will be your death,
Who you most are
And living must not be,
Your enemy.

Who can contain
The furious enemy
Or the rapt enemy
Whose death will be your death,
Whose life will be your death,
But hold his choking breath
Until he choke to stone
And you be stoned alone
In twinned and double death?

Yet brother unbeknown
Must still be alien.
And there we are lost:
We cannot put to test
Our knowledge or love.
We are pledged to be blind
By a totality of mind
Which has said: we shall learn what we already believe,

Study what we like,
Behoove what we approve,
Read our own creed
Hear our own ear

Capture our own rapture,
Making ourselves fit
To meet an enemy
And be shot by it.

What is a total mind
Fixed in a total state
But that which denies surprise
And thinks itself its fate.

What but a unity
To which variety seems
Death and inconsequence
Out of the lore of dreams.

What but united states
In which the rivers run
All one way
By an electric sun.

What but monopoly
In which villains are
Small enough to omit,
Large enough for
Major and total war.

And our monopoly
Our undivided self
With no surprise or change
No vision or remorse
No rivals and no victors
And so one enemy.

And one so total whole
Vast and incurious
Autarch and monopole
And single
Enemy.

IV

A rider to the reaches of the heart
Brings in the intolerable Russian news too late.
Careening, this pony expressman lathers his message
With fortitude and haste; and all other
Visible means of communication
Are still, are stilled.

Between the continental masses,
Between the valves of the heart
Ticks no telegraph, moves no moving picture,
Circulates no newsprint, black or white or red,
Beats no blood to believe itself thicker than water,
Rouses no breath to speak communication
From one wall to the next.
And the heart is restive,
Its chambers laboring in their disparity.

Outside the room the skies of Russia darken
Without a sign to us of any kin,
The infernal plains sever communication,
The feud of the heart strengthens itself within.
Yet it is possible somebody here may learn something,
A touch may tell, an act in hope achieve something,
A blind sky reveal something,
A heart a moment free in itself hear somewhere
A voice alien to its own to the point of amazement
Speaking a foreign tongue, speak truly—
And make in English an impossible answer
Yet true. Yet true.

THE CAMPAIGN

My Packard Bell was set up in the vacant lot near the stump
Of the old peach tree. Before it, a love-seat
In tan and green told us what comfort said.
And many looked over us, or sat on the ground, why not?
There certainly were not enough ashtrays for everybody.

And from there it began.
All down the dingle through the mustard ran the voices,
All down the shale in the sunlight ran the faces,
A board fence on the left and a board fence on the right,
Because after all this was private property.

And this is what they said:
He was a child of the people and he will be a man of the people.
He read the Bible at his mother's knee
And that Bible has followed him
All the days of his life.

This is what they said:
The sovereign state of Alabama
Gives you a leader of the people for the people
All the days of his life.
Equal educational opportunity, political opportunity, economic
opportunity,
Ability, honesty, integrity, widows and orphans.

Canal Zone deems it a privilege
To second the nomination of that great
All the days of his life.
This is what they said. This is what Cooper Blane
Representing the sovereign state of New Jersey said.

Now all the apples in our apple orchard
Are ripening toward fall
And on our poles the beans are greening fast,
The pods with sun alert.

And stubble in the field keeps springing yet
In fresh weed, white puffs of daisy weed,
The cat after the gophers
And the breeze brisk.

Round the ears of the Packard Bell brisks the breeze,
Blows the volume loud and away,
Puffs of volume pile up in the fence corners
Where the cat is active.

What do we understand?
First of all, we know the speakers are speaking the English language.
We can tell that from our love-seat, and others agree.
Second, they are both loud, lively both, and there are two of them.
Who are you for?

Now enters from the upper left, the hill slope,
A dog. After the cat.
For a while we miss the whole campaign,
But later the dog comes round for friendship.
Pats him the taxpayer and the tax receiver.

Now enters from the upper right a fisherman.
He leans to hear what's sounding on the screen,
Then wordlessly he fades
Down the green sidepatch and the cliff steps
To the roaring bay, leaving no vote behind.

Ladies and gentlemen, when I spoke to you last
In Pawtucket, Maine, the tide was coming in
With a long roar against the shingle of the world.
And ladies and gentlemen I say to you
Vote now against corruption, calumny,
Crime, evil, and corruption,
For the tide is coming in
With a long foreign roar against the world.
Against Winthrop Rockefeller, fair play,
Farm money, cartels, bourbon, and the fifth districts of the world.

Slowly comes up the moon over Lottie's rabbit shed,
Fencing into the sky its bars of protest,
But the vote Midwest moves at another cycle
Of midnight desperate.

South Dakota five no,
Robert J. Martin of the fifth district, no.
And at the four hundred and eightieth slogan
The yes and the yes that will survive the midnight.

One sure thing is
That the tough tubes on this little old Packard Bell,
Jiggling and jumping in the twi- and moonlight,
Hot as hornets in the excitement,
Won't set the beans on fire, and won't
Harm the cat, and won't
Even warm us where we sit and listen,
But will burn away
Lively as bugs in the midsummer
To get the last yes and no in the midsummer
On record to the moon's blanched countenance.
Who are you for?

SCHOOL

After the yellow school bus with the waving windows
Turned away past the corner, Sanders came over to ask,
What do you do at school? He never listened
Long, but galloped on a springtime saddle.

Where he rode, the wild ponies
Followed him in droves, so he was always responsible

And in authority, and could scarcely countenance
School, when it came the season for him.

In a crackle of blue jeans he went off to it
Waving and transportable with success,
And came back to walk fretfully over the fields, asking
What do you do at home?

INCREMENT

So populous the region
That from the next region
The crowing of children, barking of cars could be heard,
So that a continuous linkage
Of sounds of living ran
In the limber air,
District to district, Woodlake to Montclair,
Freestone to Smithfield, and one child's cry
Was not concealed from any trade route,
Or passerby,
Or upstairs island of thought withdrawn,
Or basement of submerged magnificence.
One crow
Welkined the evening sky,
Bark blasted the dark,
Like an assertion in a time of assent,
Or an increase to astonishment.

THREE STAGES

When a city undergoes disaster, it moves as a mass
Through three stages: through daze,
Then generous effort, then desperation and blame.
During all these stages, Mrs. P.T. Perkins
Lay buried under ten feet of debris, pinned down by beams.

At first she heard sirens, hoped somebody would get her out.
Later as the night wore away she surrendered her spirit,
Allowing it was all right that God take her away.

Finally what she protested to God and her rescuers was,
It was not proper that she lay there pinned under debris.

PERSONAL APPEARANCE

Out of an English mystery which a detective
Sagged through, followed by a short subject
On Cornwall, we emerged into a looping storm
Which chuckled in the gutters unexpected.

A joke. Now what we need is a nonalcoholic
Detective with an umbrella. Did you hear?
Pacing down Elmwood direct you come
Alight with laughter, nearer and more near.

Balancing a Japanese paper parasol on your thumb.
I thought you were Fulbrighting in Burma, unthought of.
Ever across this screen, outside the dark marquee,
Pass and repass the characters I love.

CURRICULUM

Knowledge of you, knowledge of all the world
Moves me and moves my sleep
And is my rattle to my fretting hand,
Knowledge of you an age I cannot live.
    I told her not to begin,
    I said rest in peace,
    I said mend your ways,
    And when the jaybirds came to the suburbs, they came in
      hundreds.

Knowledge of you, knowledge of business cycles,
Rent control and farmer legislation.
Told them to mend their ways,
Told them to rest in peace,
    And when the hundreds of jaybirds came, they came to the
      northern suburbs.

Geological ground is tempered to the spade,
An agricultural age I cannot fathom.

I told her not to begin.
And real estate is ready for expansion.
But where's the night-school course
Will count these credits up
To income tax and pre-professional Spanish?
Knowledge of all the world.
Your hundred courses.

WRECK

In the train wreck my pieces of life
Were sidewise laid to track, river, and hill,
Crosswise and palpable
To canyon and cliff.

The damage was, many later could surmise,
Insured, probable, and full of reason,
But crosswise stalled in the grave my greatest passion
Was surprise, surprise.

TALLY

After her pills the girl slept and counted
Pellet on pellet the regress of life.
Dead to the world, the world's count yet counted
Pellet on pill the antinomies of life.

Refused to turn, the way's back, she counted
Her several stones across the mire of life.
And stones away and sticks away she counted
To keep herself out of the country of life.

Lost tally. How the sheep return to home
Is the story she will retrieve
And the only story believe
Of one and one the sheep returning home

To take the shapes of life,
Coming and being counted.

VISITING HOUR

He sat in an easy chair by the open window,
Leaning back with his legs crossed.
Someone sitting on the bed was intently speaking,
And he listened intently, answering softly.

The eastern hill of houses outside his window
Flung back the sunset light into his evening,
And the smoky shadow gathered
From inside to out.

When the one who had spoken picked up her gloves and left him,
Patting his shoulder,
He came to the door of the room with her
And kissed her softly.

Then he went back to the dark sill of the window
And knelt there, head on his arms, sometimes
Softly lifting his head to look at the view, and then dropping it,
Beating it with his fists.

ORDERLY

Hysteric sparks of self in the ward of night
Jangle their light to call their care's return.
In each nook and night, each flashing brain
Asserts itself's I want.

Then what is the self of the long orderly
Who all the shift strides to the crying signs,
Strides to the foglights and the needs' unneeds
To keep the blood in vein?

His is the fire of the open hearth
Tended and mended, till the stray sparks,
Blown almost away, he brings again
To its burning brand.

TIDE

From the flood of tide to the shore edge how withdraws,
From the full consonance of waters at the brim how starves
And stands away,
How chafes and shallows upon scraping stones,
Belief, belief.

Now in the night the vessel of sea
Brims with the waters we taste in our life,
Cool to the curve and the clear
Of belief,
And runs over.

Now in the day the shocked rubble of stone
Scrapes at the ebb, and the real
Bristles of barnacle shells clash in the draining
Down of belief
Out of brine.

And I cannot learn

How in the flood of tide the shells implicit
Grate in the sand, how the rocks
Rack in the stillest full the fact of the ebb,
But in ebb
Drains down to loss the fiction of belief.

MERCURY

Then have mercy upon me.
Let one who has no care,
Sees not me there,
Likes not if he sees,
And would not, had he care,
Have mercy upon me.

He is my black mercury
Against the world's glass
To which all figures come and pass
Fair as they are in their own loving sight.
He is the black night
Which brings myself to the face of the glass.

In my indelibility
Have mercy upon me,
Quick neutral who does me forget,
Stand not
Fast at the sheer glass of my life
To make my life myself.

EXTERIOR

I never learned, did I, who you were,
What faults you, named for, lived to,
What life encumbered you,
What world's cruelties were yours—only
Your good outward and intent construction.

There's my world then, brave as you make it.
What defeats it suffers, it suffers in despite,
What harms it happens, happen like defeat
Not to your knowledge, but to one known beginning,
Your good outward and intent construction.

CARE

Most that I know but one
Make me better than I am,
Freer and more intent,
Glad and more indolent
What shall I think of you
That makes me worsen?

Is it a hate I have,
And if so, what is hate
That makes me reprobate
By expectation?
Or do I learn your lack,
Not mine, and give it back

As mine, the empty lack as mine
That makes me worsen?
And if you do misread
Me in your own need,

Why do I care whose is
The botched lesson?

Because I think if one
Should bring to my mind disdain
So near destruction,
I think that I should be
Crying out, Help me!
Help me.

CONJURE

I was sitting in what that afternoon I thought to be
The vacuum of my life,
Watching the bars of cloud darken over the housetops,
And calling to mind you, as if from far away,
As if by conjure to my lonesome wish,

When lounged in the after-school boy from down the street,
From his own vacuum, 'What's new?'
Nothing. What's new with you?
'Well, I'll tell you—' Conjure as ever
Far from the cause summons its consequence.

FOUR SONGS

1
My body is my night that sleeping lives
And in an arrogance of quietude,
Taking of nothing and not taking, gives
Lees of a lesson to be understood:

That day, in every coming singular,
Can come for neither certain help nor harm,
When the great glory patent in its star
Wakes and awakens but cannot transform.

2
Unreasonable happiness troubles me.
I look at my round face

And I see, unreasonable happiness
Is my disgrace.

My world says be angry,
And my angry hand
Turns in its palm more happiness
Than it can understand.

3
In Plato's bed I lie.
Artistically contrived,
The bed the carpenter
Made straitly as he lived
In life's utility.

Not so I use the bed,
But at a still remove
To sentence and to word
Paint it and paint it over,
As it were one I made

Not Plato's shady third.

4
In friendship feeling quiet
I spent a time asleep,
And when I woke, the marrow
Out of my bones ran out
That you were the friend I dreamt for
But not the dream I woke for.
And so I put this down for
Doubt. For doubt.

LOCATION

I set my heart out in the noontime sun,
Telling it to grow warm.
There is a space of warmth in the sky above, said my heart,
But not here.

I put my heart out by the blazing fire,
Begging it to grow warm.
There is a space of warmth on the ground below, said my heart,
But not here.

I gave my heart into your open hand,
Praying it to be warm.
There is a warm space in the world and about, said my heart,
Even as here.

DREAM

I see you displaced, condensed, within my dream,
Yet here before me in your daily shape.
And think, can my dream touch you any way
Or move you as in it you otherwise moved?

I prosper in the dream, yet may it not
Touch you in any way or may you move.
It is the splendor of the possible
Not to appear in actual shape and form.

It is the splendor of the actual
So to be still and still be satisfied,
That any else or more become a dream,
Displaced, condensed, as by my dreamed regard.

TO MAKE A SUMMER

Barney says his high-school daughter
Keeps exclaiming joy, joy.
The burden of my joy lightens
With her exclamation.

It's a generality, it takes
From my heart the sting of the singular, it sets moving
In the easy early Berkeley air
What we incommunicably share.

BROOKLYN, IOWA, AND WEST

1
I never lived behind a brick wall.
Next to brick, plaster

Seems like paper, a shoji screen
Insupportable in rough weather.

The character of brick, its autocracy,
Defines its protégées as it defends them,
Gives them a status beyond the reach of weather,
Gives them a weather beyond the reach of self.

When I came along the avenue, the rows of brick houses
Mustered to my bendable spirit, acceded
As if at six o'clock every evening I had come there
To the stations of contruction rather than to the seasons of
  change.

2
Someone watched the corn in the field—I thought it was
The sky which breathed across the silk.
Or I thought it the crow, scared crow,
Which sloped up and observed.

But no, a more illimitable eye
Stood in the dappled shade of the screen door,
Broadly watching root, blade, and ear
Each in its individual aptitude.

When I came to the screen door my Aunt Jessie saw me,
But only as a fleck in the sight of corn.
She was watching and growing, she was transforming
The shade of the porch into the growing sun.

3
Grass plunged up to the two-lane tires of cars
And to the doorstep's second step
And to the whirls
Of carousels.

It made a field a park, a wood a glade,
A store a trianon,
In stubble
A velvet double.

Grass played up around the gas pumps, woodpiles, swings,
Played the green world so green, I thought I was
A schooner in a bottle of green glass.
But it was grass.

4

A golden field has its red thresher,
Its blue sky overhead, its blue breeze.
At a great distance
Devotion moves in the field to the red machine,

Out of isolation and windy spaces, centers
To its life and wish, each one. Then a gang of threshers
Gets out on the road—you can hardly reckon
The individual master, or who serves.

5

Suddenly not plowed so deep, the seed is wind-borne,
Horses careen where cows would mull over,
Freights rattle in and out muffled
By the rocky walls and gullies, a windy crochet
Unconfirming.

The first west, as on the leaves of poplars
Dust grays and golds the deeper vein,
Dust whirls and lightens, and its thought carries
From ground to ground a surface
Like a guess.

6

To touch old snow
Frightens me, to feel
A flake settle,
Rest in my palm, and vanish
Yet rest in the rock, settle
In a tyranny of space,

So that each mountain
Commands a burden
Of ice so gross
Its features are singular in weight and stress,
Its outline as of character
Thoughtful and fateful.

When I take
Into my palm this flake
And think how long ago
It fell, and will fall,
Drifting to hand and brow,
I touch a glacial snow.

7

On the high upland plain, the boys yell in their cars,
They drive from east to west, still they are on
The high upland plain, they drive from Mac's to Barbecue,
Still they are on the high upland plain.

They yell through the small towns, finally they fall
Under the steering wheel and sleep, high
Over them drives the wheel of sky.
Still they are on the upland plain.

8

A river made up its mind at its source; nothing it met
Deeply troubled it; deflected, stalled, but not varied, it moved
Seriously down across the continent
In bountiful sunlight, freighting and purveying,
Faithful to its fountain, its following shores.

What could it believe when it came finally
Into fog, salt and deceptive, into dust
Dry and sandy, the logs, bars, nets
Shells, mixed debris, mixed decisions
Of the ambiguous ocean?

SHEEP

Led by Johns Hopkins on a trip through the heart
To the uttermost reaches of the body,
I was disappointed by X-ray and camera
At what was to be found there.

Mostly I missed the green pastures
Which I know lay on either side of the path,
The running streams of tears in their salty waters,
Their crystal waters, and the steadfast sheep.

Sheep of my heart, where do you nibble,
At the pump of the ventricle, course of the artery,
That you do not look up into the camera
To tell on what you feed?

FISH

A radioactive fish is one charged
With more of the universe that he can bear,
And in this charge he is familiar.

Through depths of our galaxy, umbrageous swells,
Coral canyons, the fish
Flicker in their schools and perish.

And we in ours flicker and are consumed
Whether or not we eat
Their bread and bait.

By too much universe we taste our diet
Enriched until
One fish, one loaf, one life is bountiful.

MONKEY

God, a man at Yale, adopted a monkey
In order to raise him up in his own image,
But only in some respects could the monk identify,
Could learn manners, but not the word of God.

Ah, always it was so, meditated the monkey dazzled and befuddled,
Out of my tree I fell in the forest of Eden,
Or if I mannerly ate, it was the wrong apple,
Or if I climbed I died.

And this is all, I guess, a semantical series
Of my ascent and fall.
His tree is not my tree, His word, my word;
His Yale, my Yale.

THE SAVAGES

As we rowed from our ships and set foot on the shore
In the still coves,
We met our images.

Our brazen images emerged from the mirrors of the wood
Like yelling shadows,
So we searched our souls,

And in that hell and pit of everyman
Placed the location of their ruddy shapes.
We must be cruel to ourselves.

Then through the underbrush we cut our hopes
Forest after forest to within
The inner hush where Mississippi flows

And were in ambush at the very source,
Scalped to the cortex. Yet bought them off.
It was an act of love to seek their salvation.

President Jackson asked,
What good man would prefer a forested country ranged with
savages
To our extensive republic studded with cities,
With all the improvements art can devise or industry execute?

Pastor Smiley inquired,
What good man would allow his sins or his neighbors'
To put on human dress and run in the wilds
To leap out on innocent occasions?

Miss Benedict proposed,
The partial era of enlightenment in which we live
Brings Dionysus to the mesa and the cottonwood grove,
And floats Apollo to the barrows of the civic group
To ratify entreaties and to harp on hope.

Professor Roy Harvey Pearce quoted,
These savages are outlandish Tartars and Cain's children,
Though someone reported once, "They do not withhold assent
From the truth set forth in a credible manner."
Is it possible?

Henry David Thoreau,
The most popular highbrow overseas reading material
For our armed forces, because while they work and wait
They see before them in the green shade
His ruddy image, said, as his last word when he died, *Indians*.

Reading today this manual of wisdom,
In the still coves
We meet our images

And, in ambush at the very source,
Would buy them off. It is an act of love
To seek their salvation.

One party to the purchase
Receipts the purchase price and hands us back
His token of negotiation which redeems:

We cannibals must help these Christians.

SISYPHUS

When Sisyphus was pushing the stone up the mountain,
Always near the top
As you remember, at the very tip of the height,
It lapsed and fell back upon him,
And he rolled to the bottom of the incline, exhausted.

Then he got up and pushed up the stone again,
First over the grassy rise, then the declivity of dead man's gulch,
Then the outcroppings halfway, at which he took breath,
Looking out over the rosy panorama of Helicon;
Then finally the top

Where the stone wobbled, trembled, and lapsed back upon him,
And he rolled again down the whole incline.
Why?
He said a man's reach must exceed his grasp,
Or what is Hades for?

He said it's not the goal that matters, but the process
Of reaching it, the breathing joy
Of endeavor, and the labor along the way.
This belief damned him, and damned, what's harder,
The heavy stone.

RECEPTION

When fate from its plane stepped down
And had its photo snapped for me in full color,
I did not know it, but it had
The hundred faces of some Christmas cards.

The severe faces of five-year-old
Wilsons and Oppenheimers, and the Pandits, the round
Fortunes of immediate Presidents
Who will not read Pascal.

Also the crazy faces of leadership
That find their goodness in their morning cup.
To whom I said, Welcome ambassadors. And they,
Which of your hundred faces calls us home?

DAVID

Goliath stood up clear in the assumption of status,
Strong and unquestioning of himself and others,
Fully determined by the limits of his experience.
I have seen such a one among surgeons, sergeants,
Deans, and giants, the power implicit.

Then there was David, who made few assumptions,
Had little experience, but for more was ready,
Testing and trying this pebble or that pebble,
This giant or that giant.
He is not infrequent.

How could Goliath guess, with his many assumptions,
The force of the slung shot of the pure-hearted?
How could David fear, with his few hypotheses,
The power of status which is but two-footed?
So he shot, and shouted!

VOYAGE

From his small city Columbus
Set sail in the floodtide of sunlight.
The boxes of buildings
Basked in secular light.

The damp interiors
Of shops on the hill streets
Dried in the golden heat,
The stairways dry and bright.

The hills stepped down in ranks
To the spacious harbor,
The whole town afforded
The patent splendor

Of the widest sundry sunshine
Over rank and section
Over room and apartment
Over court and altar.

What had then to do Columbus
With a Spanish ocean
Seamews and curlews
In a brisk brine?

But that he envisioned at its far golden
Corner another
Such a tiered city
High and dry?

MAXIM

It is said that certain orientational concepts of an ontological sort
Such as despair, sin, salvation, loneliness
Derive a certain richness from experience.

I noticed today at the Rose Bowl Parade
In the Romeo and Juliet float representing Wonder Bread,
How lonely Romeo shirtsleeved

In the frosty morning air looked, saluting
(1) the balcony made of thousands of blossoms of pink winter
  stock,
And (2) the curbstone crowd.

This won the sweepstakes prize, yet Juliet
Smiled in despair in the frosty morning air,
Receiving her certain richness from experience.

DEED

As George Washington hacked at his cherry tree,
Joseph said to him
This is the tree that fed Mary
When she lingered by the way.

As George Washington polished his bright blade,
Joseph told him
This cherry tree
Bent down and nourished the mother and her babe.

As George Washington felled the cherry tree,
Voices of root and stem
Cried out to him
In heavenly accents, but he heard not what they had to say.

Rather, he was making
A clearing in the wilderness,
A subtle discrimination
Of church and state,

By which his little hatchet
Harvested a continental
Bumper crop for Mary
Of natural corn.

RESISTANCE

A young stranger came into town looking for trouble—
Virus or seed, how could we tell quick enough?
We met immediately to map out our strategy,
And forcefully gathered in our gray beards toward the heart of
 town.

Antibodies, fighting the old fight again. Vigilant
We moved softly and effectively in upon the young stranger.
He never knew what hit him. But against him
We were not, and would never be, immune.

VACUUM

We are already on the moon,
We make such minerals in the vacuum
Furnace of the electric beam.
Their molecules together run
One every mile, in density
And pressure of the lunar cone.

In the new lab down on the waterfront
The tides of moon draw, fibers of the heart
Compress, constrict, till from this metal shape
Flows out a foil as thin and consequent
As moon on water and as moon on wing,
As moon on man the gold foil of his brain.

HEAVEN

The serpent was a risky incarnation
Which panned out badly for the human soul
Because its joy was jealous, and its ration
Incontinently post-imperial.

The couple was a daring incarnation
In the diversity of its several sin,
To seek self-knowledge, and in explanation
To argue with itself and then give in.

The martyr was a desperate incarnation
That drove its patient suffering to the wall
Bearing the tree and flesh, and in duration
Being the blasted brother of us all.

The child is an impatient incarnation
In whom aggression clamors without fear,
Self-knowledge murmurs, pathos in elation
Cries to its wide sympathos everywhere.

And now the bird is given its incarnation,
The spirit on its wing, the wing in flight,
The flight empyreal and of a station
Space-centerd, space-patrolled, and out of sight.

While it wins back to heaven, and heaven incarnate
Spins on the sphere whose light we cannot see,
Our failed flesh labors in an earthly landscape
The preconceptions of its deity.

SPEED

A light year is a cell year.
Nothing harries it on but its own speed,
Nothing halts it but its round roll.
It rushes through space as through a lifetime of incarceration.

Unconscionable to me is the speed of a light year
Which I cannot follow with my mind's eye
Or hear rushing and rattling with my heart's ear,
But stands still around me in the perpetual moment of the
universe.

In the real year into which I was born
Autumn succeeds summer and every flower
Lives hastily through the steps of its day
Filled with the clamor of seconds and happenings.

How can I fathom the millennial views
Of sky from cell walls which appertain
To eternity, when here at hand
Gardens of time happen, come into bloom, fade, happen again?

GENERATION

I saw a work so good,
Strong, delicate, and exact,
It breathed a cool wind
In a breathless day
And set the day in my heart
Like a bronze plaque.

I thought of its maker apt
In his youth to this work,
And I turned to his son to say

Thank you for him, thank him.
But did not, not to bring
To his face that shade.

I saw the sunny round
And restless warmth of the son
In his own energy rapt
To his own will, and learned
How after the father's work
We are Joseph's sons.

from

Civil Poems

1966

IDENTITY

When the third son went out
To seek his fortune,
He sought his fortune, not himself.
He knew he was
The third son.

But what his fortune was,
In what journey,
City, cave, woodland, racetrack,
Air,
Needed moving toward.

Some, I have heard, stay home.
It is the first and second
Son. They ask, Who am I?
Any answer they may get
Is premature.

CIRCUS

It seems to me that a world of hurt
Pounds at my heart. I cannot care
If this is today's sickness or tomorrow's
Prospect of fear.

So I look at a circus.
Each performer moves to entertain
On elephant, bicycle, trapeze, and high wire,
With flexible, ardent, unsharable pain.

CIVILIAN

The largest stock of armaments allows me
A reason not to kill.
Defense Department does the blasting for me
As soundly as I will.

Indeed, can cover a much wider area
Than I will ever score

With a single rifle sent me on approval
From a Sears Roebuck store.

Only the psycho, meaning sick in spirit,
Would aim his personal shot
At anybody; he is sick in spirit
As I am not.

from

Kinds of Affection

1967

When I telephoned a friend, her husband told me
She's not here tonight, she's out saving the Bay.
She is sitting and listening in committee chambers,
Maybe speaking, with her light voice
From the fourteenth row, about where
The birds and fish will go if we fill in the Bay.

The fish, she says, include starry flounder,
Pacific herring, rockfish, surf perches,
And the flatfish who come to the spawning flats
In the shallow waters near the narrow shores.
The shadow-look you know, the fish shooting
In that light green shallow, a dark arrow.

Otherwise we will get a bowling alley,
A car park and golf course, with financing,
Sift up the shallows into a solid base
With sand dredged from the deeper channels, brought in
scows
Or hopper dredges, and dumped on the fish, and then paved
over
For recreation with no cost to the city.

And so we hear the sides, the margins speaking:
To allow the Commission in the public interest
Permits for the recovery of sand and gravel
From the submerged tidelands of the state,
Fill of unlimited quality, clean sand
Replenished by the southern littoral drift;

Or yet, Dear Sirs: Your bill flies in the face
Of the U.S. Army Engineers' Barrier Study,
The Delta Study, Transportation Study,
Even the Petroleum Institute plan for bringing freighters
And hundreds of workers in to Contra Costa
To boat, bathe, drink, and return these waters.

A student I remember said to me, My mother
Wants me to be a banker, but I want to be
A sanitary engineer, spending all that money
Back toward the sea. Do you think it's possible?
See how these hills shape down back of the college
In summer streaked with little dry arroyos,
In winter running over, rush and freshet,
Through storm drains, cellars, sometimes parlors, straight
away

Down to the sea. Think of the veins
Of this earth all flowing raining water,
The drove of rivers in the pipes we've laid.

Effluent, said my student, there's a word
Give me a choice between it and *debris*
And any day I'd choose *effluent.*
Cover and fill is bleach and burn, with tires
Sticking up out of the muck, and loads
Of old brush and tree branches crisping away there.
Not for me, I like the purest water
Sparkling green under a soil, and it can breeze
Out of our pipes and chemicals, lucent as
The rain itself, around the bodies
Of fish and swimmers.

Saving the Bay,
Saving the shoals of day,
Saving the tides of shallows deep begun
Between the moon and sun.

Saving the sidings of the Santa Fe.
Saving the egret and the herring run,
Cane and acacia, mallow and yarrow save,
Against the seventh wave,

Boundary and margin, meeting and met,
So that the pure sea will not forget,
Voracious as it is, its foreign kind,
And so the land,

Voracious as it is, will not redeem
Another's diadem.
Saving the shores,
Saving the lines between

Kelp, shrimp, and the scrub green,
Between the lap of waters
And the long
Shoulder of stone.

Therein, between, no homogeneous dredge,
But seedy edge
Of action and of chance
Met to its multiple and variable circumstance.

Though a news column says that Aquatic Park is a police
headache,
In the past year, eighty-seven arrests
Of characters for crimes better not talked about,
That the lake is a favorite dumping spot for hot safes,
Burglary tools, stripped bikes, even a body,

Yet a notice says, Next week at Aquatic Park,
The V-Drive Boating Club holds its annual race—
Everybody comes out for this event—
These are the world's fastest boats, faster than hydros,
Needing the quiet water the embankment provides.

And a letter from a statistician, fond of the facts,
Compares the use of Aquatic Park to the Rose Garden: the
same pattern;
Fewest people, about five each, on a Friday of terrible
weather,
Next, about fifty, on a warm Wednesday afternoon,
Most, a hundred and fifty, on a clear windy Saturday.
Signed, sincerely, Statistician.

Some live in the deeps, a freighter
Plying between here and Yokohama.
Some live in the rose gardens,
Deeps of a street, a two-storied
Observer and participant, daily
Moving out into the traffic, back into it
Where curtains billow in their breakfast room.
The deeps. Some
Live in the margins. Have they the golden mean?

Freight whistles reach here and the fire engines
Coming from town, foundry hammers
Among the wash of waves.
Kelp drifts them up afloat, and suddenly
They are in the tinder world of lizards.
Cut ashore they bask and breathe
And then plunge back
Down the long glints that take their weight.
At home. At home. But which?

Likely a sea captain will live in a margin
But never wants to, wants a deep molded farm;
Likely an architect, but mainly weekends.
On the weekdays, along the Bay margin

Little happens, small objects
Breed and forage. Flights come in and vanish.
Solicitudes entail solicitudes.
Dredge the channel, reinforce the sea wall
And we shall have deep calling to deep directly.

She starts to speak, my friend in her light voice,
Of margins: marshes, birds, and embarcaderos.
Truths spread to dry like nets, mended like nets,
Draw in at the edges their corruptions,
To let the moving world of Bay and town
Mingle, as they were amphibian again.

Saving the Bay. Saving the blasted Bay.
That there be margins of the difference,
Scrap heap and mobile, wind ridge and ledge,
Mud and debris. That there be
Shore and sea.

A woman with a basket was walking
In the aisle of the rehearsal.
What did she carry to whom in that aisle?
Also three girls I had never seen before, though I came often
Because I had written the play.

At random scattered through the lighted
Well where the dark should be, many others
Of indefinable and nonchalant purpose.
I stared at them, but they
Did not look at the play.

One was crocheting; I've not seen crocheting
For many years. One brought a message,
A whispered conference followed, and a few went out.
There was a man reading music there
And a boy with a dog.

The intense miscellaneities and haphazard sidelines
Of the rehearsal troubled me, how they diffused
The cast's dedication to its lines.
Now look—the first-night curtain rising
Discloses as performers in this play

Boy, dog, man, music, woman with basket
Conveying what to whom on what aisle?

The mailman is coming from the next block down,
Where the sycamores thin out and flowering plums
Begin. A little boy's mother is terrified as he beats his head
On the pavement in anger. She is crying, Softer.

From the next block down, where flowering plums
Thin to industrial fog, coconut soap on the cottages,
A great morning squabble races
In which the big machines call, Softer.

One letter from the merchants' association asks:
How improve status in its concrete forms
Without demolition? How does the Vogue Cleaners
Sponge off the spot without fraying the coat?

One from the emporium of knowledge:
How can we not corrupt answers with questions
And clearly enough say to the coasting pavement,
Keep off the grass?

One from the hill: What do we do
When the formulas buckle
And men beat their heads on the pavement
In pure anger? write them a letter?

One third-class ad from the snowfields of the Sierras,
The mailman's birthplace, he says, comes cool
Across orchards to the Bay to say to his readers, Softer,
Softer.

Bodily kindness is common; though some
Kindness has no bodily motion, in some
Hand's touch of hand, foot's of ground,

Rib's of air,
The self flowers easily.

Some unkindness as of wrath can be worldly,
Brusque interiors of alienation, solid
Resistance, and a twisting hate
Of stem for stem. But close to
Paradise is the moving body of self.

Love at a distance can mean
Love of a dozen
Students sitting around for the last time
Before summer, to come no more,
Tired and sore,
Yet to be loved in their measureless aptitude.

Love at a distance can be the good
Work done by a workman, so simplified
He could not do better if he tried;
So austere, thank or praise
Only by use.
Or can be the distance at which you measureless move.

That is, far off.
So that love can be drawn
In filaments of thought, in lines as thin
As the lines latitudes rest upon.
From plenty, from perfection, marking these
Measureless distances.

After I come home from the meeting with friends
I lie to sleep on the turn of the earth as it spins
Toward the sun, toward the rising light as the day begins
And think of those I love as the day ends.

They are clearing the dishes, sweeping the ashes away,
They are threading the traffic, moving toward distances,

Disposing their hearts as the dark midnight spins,
Gathering toward the light of the new day.

Spent and regained, their strength for a cause, for a plain
Defeat or delight, strengthens my heart as it moves
Into sleep, and my sleep as it runs in the grooves
Toward the east, where a waking heart is more than mine.

In a morning of clarity and distinction
Students and I exchange questions and answers about a book
As if we had all been reading it.

Then stepping over a rough place
I hold out my hand for balance, and someone gives it.
And someone writes a letter for help I can give.

Late in the day, spare of shadow,
A camera comes to report a face
I cannot assent to; the camera

Assents. May I
Tomorrow, shady or turbulent,
Keep this day's simple fact it grants to me.

Friends in our questions, we looked together
At several mysteries,
And argued at them long and lightly, whether
Their no or yes.

Now one of us is sure, another's question
Turns counterfeit,
Unnegotiable in a redemption
By if or yet.

Wish that the future in its mysterious motion
Will come and will
Bring sureness to us all in our devotion,
But though, but still.

Who called brought to my mind the name of power,
Who loves its name.
Power.
It must not reck or rue
But does unto
As cannot unto it be done the same.

All one way move the traffic lanes of power.
It receives
Leadings, and drives them on,
Gifts and rapidly gives
Them on,
Knowing how it is giving which receives.

Happily, power in its operation
Often is given
More than it allows.
Out of its many empires, one empire,
Whether or not power knows,
Puts in its hands its one life's simple portion.

Addicts progress from saturation
To saturation, ache, thirst, slake,
To a plenitude, an oblivion, then they wake
And ache, until gradually as the sun climbs the heavens
They thirst again toward that oblivion.

Greed of the addict will intensify
And enlarge its wants beyond certainty; I
Am not so greedy; when I can be
A moment glad, repletion
Lasts me the day through, or so I say.

Nibbling greed, must I not resent
Your petty privileges, meager consent,
That certify your set of sequences?
Seek me to free you and myself from this
Addiction to a pure hypothesis.

Grievances: the warm fogs of summer
Preserve them on the bough; finally a chill
Reason sends them flying off and away.

I keep one or two and press them in a book,
And when I show them to you they have crumbled
To powder on the page. So I rehearse.

But I do not believe. I believe rather,
The stems of grievance put down their heavy roots
And by the end of summer crack the pavement.

I've been going around everywhere without any skin
And it hurts. The winds hurts. Any touch.
Attitudes distant from my own look out and find me.
When I see a face a long way off, my forehead blisters.
Raw the hot flesh under skin.

Now I am going to live so deep down in
That my skin will be a lost harm like Algeria.
Down in will be craters, violences to be tolerated
By other violences. Not by you,
Not by country or climate, this personal flaying.

Someone, an engineer, told a confab of wires
How blood flows; wove and tied the wires
To small motors. Then the pads and motors
Rode the beltline to the wholesale world.

I came in tired, crossed with enigmas,
Hextuplicate petitions, forgetting how blood flows.
Then said the engineer to his rememberer,
Go ahead, remind her, for auld lang syne.

Who shall we raise up, who glorify—our wounded,
After we have deepened and explored the wound.
He will be object of our ministration
Who needs it most as we define his need.

Tenderness, how it comes in a rush to aid us,
Like an appetite, to satiety,
After we instance to our satisfaction
The sufferer more recipient than we.

We have disarmed him, now we can help him,
Have shown him wrong, now he may seek redress.
Ready hearts, we offer to his service
The power of professional righteousness.

The doctor who sits at the bedside of a rat
Obtains real answers—a paw twitch,
An ear tremor, a gain or loss of weight,
No problem as to which
Is temper and which is true.
What a rat feels, he will do.

Concomitantly then, the doctor who sits
At the bedside of a rat
Asks real questions, as befits
The place, like Where did that potassium go, not What
Do you think of Willie Mays or the weather?
So rat and doctor may converse together.

The entrepreneur chicken shed his tail feathers, surplus
Fat, his comb, wing weight, down to a mere
Shadow, like a Graves bird ready to sing.
For him every morning
Paradise Merchant Mart reopened its doors
With regular fire sales, Shoe Parlor
Blackened its aroma, Professional

Building ran its elevators up and down
So fast that pulled teeth turned up in other mouths.

Activity. The tax base broadened in the sunlight
As gradually sun spreads wider after coffee.
It was a busy world on that side of the road,
For which the entrepreneur chicken was in his able
Way responsible.
At noon, loans, mortgages, personal interest,
At night notarized afterimages, as if by sundown
The elevator had turned to moving sidewise
Frames and phrases to be read and reread.

He was not boss or mayor, but he certainly was
Right on that spinning wheel which spun the public
In and out of his stores, and his pleasantries
Began to spin the flesh right off his bones.
That is why the chicken began to sing
High, not loud, and why transparencies
Of pipestems were his legs, his beak aloft,
His feathers lean, drawing the busy air,
And why he crossed the road.

We have the generation which carries something new not far enough,
And then the generation which carries it too far,
And then the generation which brings it back again.

Do I think of something and do you not understand it?
And does it brew along without momentum, and does finally
It take its place and move like sorghum in a slow slide

To the future, or do you yelp
Those absolutes of last degrees
Without which we are impatient? Come on! Come on!

Or do we recall a past complete, golden and still,
Toward which we tired turn and bring again
Our brilliant splendors to its ample sill?

We have the body which retells
Ontogeny through all its narrow cells,
Phylogeny through all its harrowed wills.

The life of Galileo as it is reset
On a lecture platform allows us lecturers
To step back one pace and find ourselves
Under rope or miter.

Investiture occurs not to the tolling
Of a recanting bell, merely
To our campanile striking
Its familiar schedule.

Ugly truth, lovely value take us
Into their cast, while around their
Moving inquisitions
Move the inquisitive spheres.

What do you think caused the disaster here
In 1906? Earthquake or fire?
Tremor or blaze? At least they were natural.
We did not teach them. When we were fighting them
Then we were fighting the waves.

Formerly we made Satan jump up from hell-mouth,
Rushing in black and red. We belabored him,
We beat him back. Even Faust finally
Ascended, shaking dust from his feet.
Then, not much later, we were fighting the waves.

Now our attacker in gray and silver
Is a machine. He runs scarlet ribbons
Into a tape, he manufactures
Mouth stretchers ready for screams.
Binary, he believes we are one or nothing
Though we are fighting.

We may say it was he whose faulty altimeter
Dropped Dag Hammarskjöld down over Africa.
Demon or disaster, all the same to us
Who we are blaming.
But Hammarskjöld would not. When his sons came to him
He would not fight them, he went to draw them
Free from the waves.

I fear to take a step; along the edge
Of this precipice on which we balance, bearing our burdens,
Fingers appear, clutching; they are the climbers
From below, as we were, to this ample ledge.

Maybe when we go higher, on to some plateau
Filled with flowers, we will stoop and reach
Down to their hands as once one stooped to ours.
But now I fear to step, to see the faces
Of those who take the fingers under their heels.

After noon I lie down
As if my spine were bent from burdens,
My mind from abundance,
Straitening into easy quiet.

After fifty years this is the profit,
That the weight of goods
Dozes me off. But what wakes me
Is the fright that ones thirty, twenty, are sleeping also.

They are yawning against the clatter of the day,
Its rash signs as they read them, and draw
Into a restful silence,
A sleep in the sun.

On the world's other side, the shadow
Darkest before dawn is darkening
Before dawn, and sleepers in their night
Waken with desperation for daylight.

We have it. It crackles down our freeways
As if to consume us. Is in our daylight
Someone awake enough to take, use,
Share its garish inequities?

Daniel Boone stepped up to a window
(What! A window?) with his trusty rifle,
And he shot his bear.
This was some bear.
It was a millionaire,
A Harvard, London, and a South Sea bear
A French, a football bear.

A corporate family
And incorporate party,
Thoroughly transistized
Into his rocking chair,
Built and bureaucratized,
Daddied and deared and dared,
Indomitable bear.

What an investment
Of time, of love too,
All in one body,
A computation
Of maximal purpose,
A one-man world.

Daniel is angry
That after the eighth grade
This bear should travel
So far ahead.
Unfair
That a bear
Should rock so big a chair.

So gets him, and as he is got
Shows him
Shows us
It takes no complicated bomb or plot
To win again us back to wilderness,
But just one pot, pure, individual, shot.

As difference blends into identity
Or blurs into obliteration, we give

To zero our position at the center,
Withdraw our belief and baggage.

As rhyme at the walls lapses, at frontiers
Customs scatter like a flight of snow,
And boundaries moonlike draw us out, our opponents
Join us, we are their refuge.

As barriers between us melt, I may treat you
Unkindly as myself, I may forget
Your name as my own. Then enters
Our anonymous assailant.

As assonance by impulse burgeons
And that quaver shakes us by which we are spent,
We may move to consume another with us,
Stir into parity another's cyphers.

Then when our sniper steps to a window
In the brain, starts shooting, and we fall surprised,
Of what we know not do we seek forgiveness
From ourselves, for ourselves?

In the town where every man is king,
Every man has one subject,
Every man bends to his own foot.
Bring on the mirror that he may properly bend.
But who will bring it on?

In the castle where is no hunger and no need,
Every man gives gifts and receives
Gifts. But of these only his own
Enhance him, the ring giver.
He must wear his ring.

Gradually, as he resolves the oppression of his edicts,
Losing his fellow lords to dim perspectives,
Monoliths of rock and stone, even
Of reinforced concrete, become before him
Mirrors. He licks the glass.

Throwing his life away,
He picks at and smells it.
Done up. When did I do this up?
I date its death to the time someone
Said something.
Back then.
Everything else, all striving, making,
Marrying, error,
Is this old bird.

Pah! He throws it.
As the long string lengthens
Out of his hand,
It begins unwinding
The ligaments of his hand.

So you are thinking of principles to go on,
Principles of controversy, Alexander Meiklejohn says,
Sitting in lamplight briskly, as late November
Collects about him. Well, I will give you one.
One is enough. Coherence.

Coherence of agreement and difference,
Wave and particle, concept and image,
Exuberant complement I give you, not contrary,
To keep a precarious gritty life between chaos
And bland entropy, in which we can prevail.

Our mien of survival, to know our separate natures
And allow them. Allow
Dividing light. Let be
Candle and galaxy; the first word of them, logos,
The wish to be.

Alec, agreed. The soft rain quickens
In the increasing twilight. But what about fights?
What about sorties, annihilations,
Eyeball-to-eyeball confrontations,
And competition in the life of trade?

Why, a game needs rivals and a rival makes
The world green. But grant a plain clash

In a single world, true contradiction, then it rests
Upon degree, remoteness
Of one sight from another within that world.

I say I see a blue jay on the roof
Across the way. You do not. Do I contradict you?
Then I come to stand where you stand,
Use your eyes, see what you see, a blue pipe.
But yes from where I was, it looked like a bird.

Bird, a good name for a small blue object
On a roof. Does it flutter, stir?
Even if it did, you might say
That's not a bird, not much of a bird I mean,
In my country are real birds, bluer than that.

To live a life out is to learn the ways
Of action in which we undertake the reach
Of knowing. The different lines of fact
To follow out, to cling to, when the sense
Of footing falls away.

To know where we are free and where determined,
So not to imprint one feather on another,
To know how the bees of atoms hum in the table,
A universe of spaces,
Yet steady our glasses on their giant wings.

To know the world within, and there confound
Self-contradiction in its knot of splendor,
And let its science say,
You are a committee, meet and negotiate,
Te auton.

Alec, myself I meet, but in what meeting?
Of many meetings? Of error, say? Well, push
The wrong-way car back over the line before impact.
Of planned aggression? Then try to intensify
The hoped-for suffering, to its desirers.

Of rare real contradiction? Then discover
The differences of degree that separate
One view from the other, and so celebrate
The fortunate variance, the happy fall,
And light to contemplate the difference by.

The trouble stirs at the limits of a life.
Mind starts in the dark to see what it can see,
Its hope marked plainly in nucleic code.
The bear goes over the mountain, and next day
Roams out of Eden entirely.

I seek fullness, I seek the complement
Of all I know, and it will not be still.
It will beget Abel and Cain if you will,
Who will say, Complement is a rarity;
We are engaged upon diversity.

Mediation has taken its move forward.
It notes not the surfaçe arrogance
But the underlying regard.
The long destiny moving toward birth.
It can tell free speech from bound action.

It meets and holds the long birch love of goodness,
The long birch taste of guilt.
It takes the fierce birch blush of conscience
Into the open world in price of power,
Asking its name and even enemy.

Discourse makes signs to us, all signs of trouble,
To come between us and obliteration.
Trouble preserves the world and tells its name
Stemming from early day,
From early night.

Alec, the night comes in
Upon the lamp, and you determined and free
Open the door to it and bring it in. We're late,
The telephone rings, trouble on every hand
Seeks your agility, and makes you smile.

From Hindi:

I. A star quivered in a corner of the sky.
I thought, yes
everything sometime or other will shine out like this.

A pebble stirred
the water of the drowsy waves.
I knew
at least for once inertia will be shaken.

Blossoms flowered
in the deeps of forests,
their fragrance spoke out, yes
once at least I scatter and bestow.

What more to ask
than images of my aspiration—
but belief needs none,
a dream is better;
what can an image do but shine or scatter,
what will it offer?

—"A Star Quivered," by Kirti Chan-huri

II. . . . But the accursed twilight came,
brought with it the bad spirits of past memories
and a shabby dusk.

All of a sudden, as if wet fuel started smoking,
as if that sort of smoke rose up from the houses
in a spiral, with a dark hazy line behind it,
mind and eyes burned with bitter tears.

This twilight, with somewhere a patch of light
but mostly darkness prevailing,
increased, as if building a fence of giant size
for a giant with no heart.
I felt that my life was in a cage
with ostriches, tigers, bears, wild dogs around me,
my life inextricably set in the accursed twilight.

—"You Are Alone," by Ajit Kumar

III. My father,
a conquered Everest,

my mother,
an ocean of milk poisoned with poverty,

my brother,
a lion cub cinched up as a pack animal,

my sister,
a doll made out of soiled clothes,

and I,
a kettle of water
boiling away to vapor,
water consumed into vapor.

—"The Family," by Vishwanath

Looking over toward Tamalpais,
I could see cars crossing its Sunday shoulder
Over to picnic. Metal by metal
Scratched the light, moved clear over
And I would join them.

Then a wind rose, a dun cloud
Came across, and I thought quickly
How to treat a house in a tornado?
Close down tight, crouch in a corner,
Or open up the doors and let her ride?

The cloud was in the house, a crowd of shouters,
A kind of club on an outing over this way.
Rushing, protesting, they kept saying
Where's the rest of the house, where's the rest of it?
Sundays of the kind they used to be.

Along the street where we used to stop for bread,
There used to walk
A leathery megalomanic dwarf, playing
At directing traffic.

Up we would drive and park, and I would promise
Every time to say hello to him,
But did not,
Nor did his wild eyes ever look,

But snap and spark,
And the best I managed

Was a pale smile in his direction,
Which was nowhere.

That leathern skin, pinched eye, dumb jaw
I saw, I see, in the somewhat deprived,
And every time I am heartsick to claim it.

And so am reasonable, yes indeed, but of course, to be sure.
Oh rebels against reason, where do you fly?
To my wild dwarf on his drug? I will have him greet you.

Dear Frank, Here is a poem
I dreamed of you last night;
It makes me happy
Because it makes sense to me.

We went to the Greek Theater to see a play
And as we entered were given elaborate menus
Of the players' names.
Dinner was three dollars.
It was served on the little round tables from cocktail lounges.

I kept leaning back against your knees,
Because of those backless benches, and you kept moving
Farther and farther away in the amphitheater,
I following, until finally you said,
Jo: I am having the six-dollar dinner.

Still early morning, the wind's edge
Catches in veins the edges that stick in them;
Thorny friends, burrs of confusion,
Pressures of office that take a rhomboid wrench
Through every breath. I would, I say,
To the genii that live in the long lamp of hope,
Have them all rounded, is that not possible?

All edges rounded till they will bubble
Easily together? Slowly the sun,

Rising up over the roofs and trees,
Brings another way beyond my wish.
The edges meet and fit, the angles turn
To complement, merge and sparkle, vein to vein,
As the sharp morning seeks delineation.

When Sanders brings feed to his chickens, some sparrows
Sitting and rocking in the peach tree at the fence corner
By the chicken house fly up
And shoot off to another tree farther away,
An acacia. The whole air
Is shaken by their mass motion.

But then one leaf of the empty peach tree stirs
And I see in it one sparrow sitting still.
Is he a guard? absentminded? averse
To mass motion? Rather, he may enjoy
The comings and goings
Of Sanders to the chickens.

Apart from branches in courtyards and small stones,
The countryside is beyond me.
I can go along University Avenue from Rochester to Sobrante
And then the Avenue continues to the Bay.

Often I think of the dry scope of foothill country,
Moraga Hill, Andreas, Indian country, where I was born
And where in the scrub the air tells me
How to be born again.

Often I think of the long rollers
Breaking against the beaches
All the way down the coast to the border
On bookish cressets and culverts blue and Mediterranean.

There I break
In drops of spray as fine as letters

Blown high, never to be answered,
But waking am the shore they break upon.

Both the dry talkers, those old Indians,
And the dry trollers, those old pirates,
Say something, but it's mostly louder talking,
Gavel rapping, and procedural dismays.

Still where we are, and where we call and call,
The long rollers of the sea come in
As if they lived here. The dry Santa Ana
Sweeps up the town and takes it for a feast.

Then Rochester to El Sobrante is a distance
No longer than my name.

When the sun came, the rooster expanded to meet it,
Stood up, stirred his wings,
Raised his red comb and sentence
Rendered imperative utterance
Saying, Awake. Nothing answered.
He took in a beakful of air; yes, first it was he,
And engendered a number of hard-shelled cacklers,
One for each day in the week.
They grew in their yard, the dust in their feathers,
Who heard them praise him? An egg.

In the night, in the barn, the eggs wakened and cried,
Saying, We have been wakened,
And cried, saying Father, so named him,
His feathers and beak from the white and the yolk.
Father, who newly can ring out the welkin,
And crow, we will listen to hear.
As toward him we move, and the wings of our feathers grow bright,
And we spring from the dust into flame
He will call us his chickens.
But that was already their name.

How goes a crowd where it goes?
Ten or a dozen, along a road?
Each wavers.

Some ramble on the road's shoulder,
Some lean in, brush or confer, confidential,
Some hold the center as it marks the way.

Which is the group's line to its exact
Destination? The ramblers
Have to disclose it.

The leaf is growing,
But not before your eyes like a motor scooter,
Because it is still,
More like a hand than a stone.

What about stone?
It is growing
Before your eyes like a motor scooter,
Not like a leaf but a hand.

A hand? In it are growing
A leaf and a stone, and grow still
From the hand when it's gone,
Buzzing off like a motor scooter.

Does the world look like a park to you? Yes, almost suddenly
The world looks like a park.
Are there worn spots in the shorn grass? Yes, under
The childrens' feet,
And under the feet of bison behind trees.

Are there temperature controls in the park? Yes, the warm sun
Is made shady, and the warm shade
Sunny. Feelings too,
Whether out on the shorn lawns or behind the bushes,
Run hot and cold to the edges of Africa and Chicago.

It is a national park, then? Yes, national
In its red, white, and blue bunting, in its scope and convenience.
Hear the bears groping for sliced bacon.
In the national parks, however, the turbulence
Still perseveres, of waters?

Glaciers and gorges move down to the warm lawns?
Yes, but just to the point where the dams take them. Then
they ripple
Over the flooded farms of the Havasupai,
Of Nefertiti and Osiris,
And carry them softly off to the park's museums.

Every day when she came to the steps that led
To the class to be taught,
The bells in the tower were telling the cost of the hour,
And there they met.
They were ready and she was ready.

One day, by a lost minute or so, she came
To the silent spot
Where she waited the bells to ring and they did not,
The future fallen bells, but had flown
Into a past over and done.

Where had the unsounded hour gone?
It was ready and she was ready.

I am trying to think what it means to be right.
I am trying to think what good means,
Goods mean.
I have come from the uncertainties of childhood, school, and
foreign travel
To my familiar husband, daughters, and sons,
In my familiar low-lying home alight with flowers
And my beige car and hair.
Why am I good?

Because I have worked with intensest devotion,
With patience unstinting, seldom with anger,
And with a tremendous strain at understanding
Toward this purpose: toward these good sons,
Shining daughters, husband content.
How does the world corrupt them past my hand?

I wake at the third alarm that the dawn will never
Come again, that in some terror
The bedstead will overthrow the light.
In forced lamplight I wander among the sofas
And read headlines of the death of God.
God, you have stood
By my side, you have held my hand
From cruelties,
You have guided my steps
In the gentlest ways,
You have said to my heart, rest.
Work and rest. Love and rest.

Now you move off, where?
Leaving at my side, in my garden furniture,
Many lives other than mine, who do not know me
And I do not know them.
You bring me into the heart of my living room
And you open a window on a world
In which it was not built.
The flames that burn me
From some hurled cocktail,
From some sick son, other son?
From some soft southern voice, soft Asian robe,
Burn them, by a choice I cannot conceive.

Are you evil as well? You leave
Heaven in spite
And then rise back to it with coal on coal,
Casting the heavy flames on carpet floors?
If my old father, my happy husband were you,
If I were you,
Could we not keep goodness for our good,
Could we not
Let others, when they will, trade with hell,
The neighbors' boy, the citizens of the left,
All trouble seekers, let them seek
And find, but not in heaven?

Heavenly color
In television strikes the colors of blood,
The screen burns among trees during dinner.
The dog that worries for Associated Gas
Assumes the presidency.
Now I must lay me
Again to sleep, the soul you take to keep
Youthful still, trembles.
The yard outside, world outside cry.
If it is right and good
Where you are,
Why are you not here?

Bucking and rolling, the ship bent
Over the curve of the world,
Round, round, the gulls flapped,
Sails flapped,
Round, they called out to Columbus, as cinnamon
Filled the imaginative Atlantic air.

The speechless microscope of Hooke opened
Cells of cork, not calling but being round,
The dense
Peripheral regions of its cytoplasm
Round the watery vacuoles,
The sweet breath of oxygen over sugar.

Round, says a life, rustle of dividing life,
Upon the curve
Of morning's coming back,
A morning first to see one thought turning
In expectation
Its aromatic line.

In the neighborhood of my childhood, a hundred lungers
Coughed in their tents like coyotes.
The sand was dry and saged with mesquite.
Even so, from mountains the dew dropped
Down on the canvas in the early dark.
The kerosene puffed away as I fell to sleep.

In that rich landscape I was deprived,
Because no negro coughed among the tents, moved
Outward among the distant orange groves.
A square shot of Indians walked the coals,
But so pure the absence of black skin, I thought
All the sorrows of the world were white.

Later, a stonewall neighbor Harriman's
Krazy Kat neither spoke to us, nor spoke
To any negro neighbor because we had none.
Mexican squatters in the boxes in the dry river
Sent no drift of blackness to our dream.
Black Sambo was our child.

When land gave no relief, across the plains
The white and blistered figures in jalopies
Moved into town, but did not come to college.
And so who were they? Such an array
In sandy paleness needed to be brown.
Minority, myself.

Deprived.
Out of the sunny and the shadowy scenes
Where I look back with wonderment and love,
An oversimple marginal deployment
Of absence,
A relentless letting be.

Down from another planet they have settled to mend
The Hampton Institute banisters. They wear bow ties and braces.
The flutings they polish with a polished hand.

Wingless, they build and repair
The mansions of what we have thought to be our inheritance.
Caution and candor they labor to maintain.

They are out of phase. I prepare
To burn all gentle structures, greek or thatch,
Under the masterful torch of my president here and abroad,

Till stubble outsmolders, and muslim and buddhist crack
In the orbit of kiln.
                                        A smoke
To some calm Christian plant will drift,

To where they are mending their mansions, beside of whose
  doors
They are standing at ease, they are lifting the fans
Of unburdenable wings.

Yesterday evening as the sun set late,
    We parked at Land's End, past the Golden Gate,
    To see the cypress lean in from that ocean,
    And the wave path lengthen to the lengthening sun.
    In the VW over beside us, a yellow-haired girl
    Looked at us with a radiance
    Hardly receivable. We smiled and turned
    Back to the sea as she held out her arms to us.
    Her blown voice said to the three with her,
    I know why you brought me here,
    To love these mixed-up people, and I do!
    See, they are smiling at me, poor sad
    Mixed-up people! Her friends sheltering
    Walked with her to the cliff's edge.
    Deep to the rocks, far to the falling sun,
    She reached her hand. She saw her hand,
    Head it close to her eyes, widened its fingers,
    Hand translucent. Who will keep it? She put it
    Inside the coat of the yellow-haired boy and he leaned
    Over her like the wind.
    When she came back to the car she had lost her hand,
    Lost us. We said goodbye as they drove off.
    A trawler crossed between us and the sun.

When I was eight, I put in the left-hand drawer
Of my new bureau a prune pit.
My plan was that darkness and silence
Would grow it into a young tree full of blossoms.

Quietly and unexpectedly I opened the drawer a crack
And looked for the sprouts; always the pit
Anticipated my glance, and withheld
The signs I looked for.

After a long time, a week, I felt sorry
For the lone pit, self-withheld,
So saved more, and lined them up like an orchard.
A small potential orchard of free flowers.

Here memory and storage lingered
Under my fingerprints past retrieval,
Musty and impatient as a prairie
Without its bee.

Some friends think of this recollection
As autobiography. Others think it
A plausible parable of computer analysis.
O small and flowering orchard of free friends!

Have I outgrown you?
Have we lived in a little city together
And now while you map your local entertainments
Do I go out upon some new portage,
Desperate to be lonelier and beyond,
Wealthier to ascend?

You write that things are going well in town and I see them
Going well. But by what luminant?
Bobby, see Jane jump; Eve, Adam. Clearly
Temptation brings the light so full to bear
That you and semblance have the same substance.
Am I going away to your nearest distance?

from

Fields of Learning

1968

FIELDS OF LEARNING

When we go out into the fields of learning
We go by a rough route
Marked by colossal statues, Frankenstein's
Monsters, AMPAC and the 704,
AARDVARK, and deoxyribonucleic acid.
They guard the way.
Headless they nod, wink eyeless,
Thoughtless compute, not heartless,
For they figure us, they figure
Our next turning.
They are reading the book to be written.
As we start out
At first daylight into the fields, they are saying,
Starting out.

In every sage leaf is contained a toad
Infinitely small.

Carbonized grains of wheat unearthed
From the seventh millennium B.C. town of Jarmo
In the Tigris-Euphrates basin
Match the grains of three kinds of wheat still extant,
Two wild, one found only in cultivation.
The separate grains
Were parched and eaten,
Or soaked into gruel, yeasted, fermented.
Took to the idea of bread,
Ceres, while you were gone.
Wind whistles in the smokey thatch,
Oven browns its lifted loaf,
And in the spring the nourished seeds,
Hybrid with wild grass,
Easily open in a hundred days,
And seeded fruits, compact and dry,
Store well together.
They make the straw for beds,
They ask the caring hand to sow, the resting foot
To stay, to court the seasons.

Basil: hatred: king over pain.

What did you do on the last day of day camp?
First we did games, running around and playing.

Then we did crafts, making things.
Then we did nature, what goes on and on.
Eventually a number
Of boys have got big enough
Through all the hazards of drag-racing, theft, and probation,
To start for junior college, two transfers away,
Mysterious as Loch Ness.
While of grandmothers a number
Have stooping arrived to seventy or eighty
And wave the boys on, shaking
With more absentminded merriment than they have mustered
In half a century.

King Henry the Eighth consumed many daisies
In an attempt to rid himself of ulcers.

Algebra written across a blackboard hurts
As a tight shoe hurts; it can't be walked in.
Music, a song score, hurts,
How far lies one note from another?
Graft hurts, its systems of exploitation
In cold continuance.
Argosies of design, fashions to which the keys
Rest restlessly in an Egyptian tomb.

In every sage leaf is contained a toad
Infinitely small.

BOTANY

Farthest from town's the rocky shore,
The coastal strand. Beaches of sand
Carried by surf grasses keep the tides.
Dunes built out of sand verbena
And sand crabs run from the waters
As grunion run, as moonlight, sandlight.
The marshes move and take a life.

Monterey aphis and midge darken the sorrel.
Riparian woodlands move into patches of canyon.
Come into cultivation, cropland and pasture;
To the eucalyptus groves of the subdivisions
Barn owl and sparrow hawk;

To Rural Free Delivery and Union Square,
Who only?

Some populations, as of Bermuda grass and strawberries,
Are interconnected by vascular systems
Not wholly individual.
By gene exchange the local population
Is the surviving unit, an array
Of individuals each with different tolerances
Of wind or of drought.

Plants on mountains, dwarfed and easy-flowering,
Persist when transferred to quiet gardens.
Lab jar to rain forest, a spatial energy.
Alpine sorrel as it respires through snow
Grows leaves for food, blows fertile seed
Into the summer crevices of slopes, wanes,
Flowers, and breathes again through snow.

Trees choose a spar or hull high in the forest.
Who chooses cellophane, charcoal,
Or the seventy flowers of a saffron pond?
Who the alkaloid
Sugar of poppy, purple of atropine, blade of papyrus,
When the terrible case of disease is of life,
To cure it of life?

PHYSICS

The mean life of a free neutron, does it exist
In its own moving frame a quarter-hour?
In decibel, gram, ohm, slug, volt, watt, does it exist?
Not objects answer us, not the hand or eye,
But particles out of sight.

Does a book in equilibrium on a shelf
Compose its powers? It upsets my mind.
Turbulent flow, function of force times distance,
The sledge with a steel head
Is energy transformed.

Illusion boils a water into cold,
A speed of pulse slows by chronometer,

A camera's iris diaphragm opens wide
To faint light. Lenses
Render to us figures equivocal.

Sight in its vacuum, sound in its medium strike so aslant
The thunder relishes a laggard roll,
And as long waves of low-pitched sounds bend around corners,
Building-corners cut off a high wrought bell,
To set its nodes and loops vibrating symmetrically at the surface.

Neutron transformed, neutron become again,
In glass and silk, tracing a straight world line,
Exists in its gravitational electromagnetic fields
Trembling, though beyond sight,
Initially at rest.

PATHS

Going out into the fields of learning,
We shake the dew from the grasses.
All is new.
The paths we make through the wet grasses shine
As if with light.

They go where we take them, where they go.
Slow wings unfold, scarcely any
Motion happens but our heavy seeking.

Ant labors, hopper leaps away; too early for the bee,
The spider's silk hypotheses unfold
Tenacious, tenable.

from

To All Appearances

1974

THREAD

Take an emotion, how can it be?
I cannot do crochet
But take a doily—
The white threads in and out
In, say, a shell,
Loop and lock
Filling out this doily.
It would protect a curved back of a chair velour
From a neck velour.

Now the emotion: where the white thread
Should continue itself into its measurement,
Doily of heart diffidently skips
Becomes a repeat of pearls or this or that
A purple thread as of the outset purple.
You crazy feeling
Let the hard line bask
On simple pattern, not your prying
Arabeques of what? flesh? watercolor?

HOW I CAUGHT UP IN MY READING

After the season was summer
And students were rocked in their summer cradles,
I began to catch up.
First I read many accumulated magazines
On the President's unemployment commission, for example,
And revelations about Senator Dodd.
Wasn't he dead?
Then I read
A number of old novels like *Anna Karenina*
And a number of new science fictions,
Then I read
Your thesis and Betty's thesis and Clinton's
Thesis
And advised alterations
In marginal notes of great thickness.
Then I read the Berkeley *Daily Gazette* and the recipes
In *Better Homes*. Then
I read a lot of poems, all the pamphlets in the house, hundreds

piled up, friends and strangers, poems. And answered. And replied.
Then
I looked around
And read one poem
Again
Again.

CONSERVANCIES

Plums on the ground
Lay with a soft sound
And the sweet sense of dissolution they have.
She used to pick them up
With a scoop, thickened with bees.
She would carry away into bottles what she could save
And the cinnamon worked in the kitchen
Saying *save.*

Now when the lingering fresh breezes
Flurry in the field rows
Some sifts of clear summer air,
She pickles the puffs in clear jars,
Brings them out
In winter scarcity,
Gives everybody on his plate of melathion
A rich spoonful of air.

TRACT

Old tract, the houses of wood siding
Old callas at the drainpipes, a frontal
Cedar, line among lots
Cabs, a wagon, a pick-up
And the bay not far, a dozen miles over town.
A boy on a bike now and again
Makes up a tunafish sandwich and starts off.
Few go out otherwise, they stay in to listen.

For some tracts, a whole range
Of mountains takes the bay's place,
Holds all the answer or loss
Behind curtains as tears.
For some, beyond the outskirts of the houses,
More callas, more houses.

NEW TRACT

Streets under trees
    lamps in their windows
    gathering dark,

Comfortable coming of home,
    fussing and crying, tears of the tired, yet lamplit
    windows under the trees,
    trees under opening stars.

Work done, car in the port,
    children cleared and asleep under stars,
    why not enough?

Held in the hold of the mountainous night
    And the bend of the street,
    why not enough?

Building and bearing
    street after street in the town to the mountains and on,
    state after state in trees of the plains with a plenty or spare

    and by rivers
    why not enough?

Later from night
    trees upon street
    droop of the dark sides, haggard of morning,
    show that it was.

VISIT

Cricket complained quite a bit how lights wept falling
In and out her wings

Stars in her eyes
Dimming.

Bear
Took the market approach
Up and down.
Brrr, said cricket.

In his strong voice
Bear talked all around her
Built the place she was in
Ordered up sweet rolls, had to go.

You take care now, bear said.
Bye, bye son, said cricket.

IF YOU WILL

Shall I pull the curtains against the coming night?
No, there is still a fine sun in the treetops; let them be.
All right, now it is darker; shall I now
Close out the dark? You will close out the light.
All right; how quick the dark comes. But see how the moon
Floods as it floods the earth even this room.
Moonlight, it's time to sleep, shall I draw now
Curtains against the cold? It's summer weather.
Shall I? Yes, if you will; the light will pass.
It is your life that stands beyond the glass.

RETROSPECTIVE

Once I didn't think that much about making the bomb.
In the halls I turned
Away from the machinists who made it,
I said sorry
To Japanese friends, especially one from Hiroshima
I agreed with in liking Isaac Walton.
Not thinking of the dead as death makers,
I said doubly in my heart about nightfall
May there be peace again.

Then a quarter-century of Chaucer went very fast,
Now in one way, by a foreshortened view and exaggerated,
I have lived to the time in this free city where I say,
Look what I have been doing,
I have been making the bomb, creating,
Letting be created, the following real people:
John Mitchell, General Westmoreland,
Sheriff Madigan, John Mitchell,
The list keeps sticking so it doesn't get to the bit names.

Jump: is Nasser mine? And Ky mine?
Somebody asks a syllabus for the next quarter:
How to keep from making
John Mitchell, General Westmoreland.
Composition: to think again
To work again the slow used-over clay.

WITNESS

Gassed going between classes
Students said little,
Huddled their books and ran.
As helicopter crews waved down low at them
They were silent,
Yelled and were silent.

Now the trees speak, not running or reading
But with cast leaves tallying
The cost of a gas deterrent.
My throat alive still cries,
But how to tell without dying
Is not told by the dying trees.

MY FEAR IN THE CROWD

The thousand people stand in the sunlight,
They are taking in the messages of the speakers
Deliberately, they are weighing the judgments,
They are making up their minds.

The sun is on their shoulders, weight of the earth,
They know it, and they are not despairing.
Against odds, they may consider quietly and freely
What they will do.

Who knows then, not I,
And I am desperate in no knowledge,
If later, somewhat dispersed, they will yell
And turn and burn the place where they stood.

But look, the May light
Outlines each shape, each moving
Out from the crowd, each carrying
In his own mind the place where he stood.

VIEWS FROM GETTYSBURG

Students all, we sit on the ridge, in a Pontiac GTO.
The western hills are blue in the haze of noon,
The near woods dense and cool, a breath of wind
In the wheat rippling toward us,
Fences cutting
An angle at the peach orchard, very quiet.

One or two small boys off at a distance
Man a gun emplacement; up through the wheat
Toward them come in the smoke and flash of fire
The faces of the Confederate dead, boys also.
They come right into the cannister shot,
They look up to us as they come in bunches, their flags
Surging and dropping.

Where is the vantage? Vantage from depth mistaken
Or height assumed?
Faces look up into deflective glass
Responseless, downward to a beveled screen,
Windshielded both. Where is the voice to answer?
Where the fair fight?

*   *   *

Northern General Meade, we are looking for you
In the suburbs. Now it is summer,

Sailboats in the lagoons slip gaily,
Bourbon barrels in arcades, brigades of houses
Come over costly ridges for the view.
General Meade holds position, not confused
By wrenched faces fighting as they come.

Back in town, as the clock strikes one,
A math professor takes up his math class,
And I am eating, for the first time,
A sweet-sour mix of Pennsylvanian
Apples and hocks, hot as the day is.
Up from the valley
Keep coming white faces into volleys of thunder.

We are in some kind of fight for or against with the Union army.
Tired and footsore in the GTO,
Ready for a quick look at the news and to bed,
We sit staring into open faces.
There they come again, kooks now,
Straight in the camera fire, rebel yells,
Expressions fixed and wild.

Lianas, ropes of jungles, death defying,
Caves, thatches, trapped pits, a guerrilla
Concept of fever, a white Ghanian
Hill bungalow beyond the plain
Grasses of Gettysburg. General Meade,
What is your command
As we look downward?

It's a clear view up here from the fourth story
Of a Telegraph Avenue apartment. When the crowds rise
Between the level bakeshops and the drugstore
Their white eyes are clear.
Where is the mace or free beer to stop them?
They are looking with horror to a height like this one.

* * *

Let me alone, do you hear,
I am whole and sound,
I will stay that way,
I am walking along
The road to Emmetsburg in the wrong direction.

Or, pile up my guts in my hand
And I will carry them
Up to the stone wall at its angle and over it
To silence just one cannon.
I speak into its mouth: Silence!
Most of the brigades go together,
Suffer thirst, cheer. They pick up the banner and follow together.

Night in the Blue Ridge, Corrington's boys are returning
From their visit to the battlefield.
They are winding along those heights,
See nothing below them,
But the west is widening the white of its eye.

* * *

Traveling, or going on, or in pursuit,
A wheel will hit a bend in the western grade, and then below
Evening in the river trees, among clusters
Of roofs, and one spire
White in the twilight, ready as memory.
Many the tired night, late lamps, rays scattered
Over the leafy spire, husbanding light.

But how do I see past this bend again,
Southern fields
Wide and open, full fields, no town,
Where do I turn?

Over the shoulder, up at the hill crest
High in the late sun, the maple cluster
And the town cluster round its spire. Up there,
Head back, eyes lifted,
Tired I come to you, Is it home, I must ask, master,
Is it father, lord?

* * *

From the lectern angle, the lecturer
Waits, watching,
Ready to fire,
Holds till he sees
The whites of their eyes,
Then lets them have it—
Instruction, quick from the holster,

Low and steady,
At a little angle.
They take it well,
Heads toward writing fists
Ducked in deflection,
Bent elbows dispersing
Ninety-pound jolts of information
Over a wide radius.

* * *

I was a soldier not for money or office.
I was young, single, physically able,
And my country was assailed.
West and north of the Spangler House, on low ground,
Pickett for Lee took up, according to G. R. Stewart, the tactic of
Napoleon.
A direct rush under cast-iron ball and shell,
Rending the limbs of oak trees.

A few hundrd went forward under Armistead.
There she goes! The deep and steady roar.
The blue-bellies ran from the Angle and the flags went backward.
The ground was fairly jammed with Pickett's men
In all positions, lying and kneeling.
Back from the edge were many standing and firing
Over those in front. Every foot of ground was occupied
By men engaged in mortal combat
In every position possible under arms.

There was a sudden swinging of clubbed muskets,
Not bayonets. Everything trembled in balance.
A general said, Will you see your colors storm the wall alone?
A general said, The best the men can do
Is to get out of this. Let them go.
Thrusts, yells, blows, shots, and undistinguishable conflict,
The strange resistless impulse moved them.

Throwing of stones: the local traprock weathers
Into chunks conveniently sized and shaped.
It takes half a minute to load a rifle,
So throwing stones is faster.
Where are the men who fought us, losses five to one?
A rooster must fight best on his own dunghill.
Did you see any Massachusetts or New York regiment

Come down and run over the 72nd?
I'd like to meet the man who said it!

A man by the name of Metz, belonging to my company,
Fought his way back to it, and said,
I thought that if I were to get killed
I would like to be near somebody who knew me.
He fell across the stone wall, crossways.
Three o'clock.

*   *   *

From an apartment high-rise or steep residential
Hill, the regiments
Of visible houses are implacable.
Contemplate one broken line
Multiplied, and there's no day for you.
Night has a different portion, then the stars
Astronomize a heaven to earth and give you
Peace from the other side of understanding.

So it is day, noon even, when the houses
Turn, take up their arms,
Flash in the gunsmoke fog
Signals to say they'll have the ridge by sundown.
Forty floors down, you see them looking toward you,
Marshaled
From coal beds far under peach orchards
Yelling what? It is hard to hear them.

*   *   *

Along the veins of coal a life is lived,
Half standing, lying,
Half breathing, smothering.
Black to the core and to the whites of eyes.
What are those lanterns glimmering?
The weight of wealth of earth sometimes lets up
To sleep at night, collapses others.
A steady craft, capable at five years,
Informs its pride.

An astronaut intensively informed
Reclines to head room
Along the veins of space, its folded brain.

Thinks, thinks in there,
Does calculations,
Comes out to walk, goes back to breathe,
Stifled among his rations. He is up and away.
And coal somewhere, even at that airless extremity,
Keeps him, gives him his life.

* * *

Softly the capitol hill surveys its scene,
The roads of its marble caverns
On which it governs,
Litter of tombs.

Each stone figure put to sitting
Upon his grave
Faces outward, skyward and sunward,
Thinking to live.

Underground, whoo, whoo, something is coming,
That's the ticket,
Straight up the aisle breaking the silence
Dirt flies out of the railway tunnel.

On the other side of the track and valley
Tracking his hole,
The old mole is busy upchucking
A new hill.

We will build up the hill and come up so the white of the eye
Will be lambent and clear
At our height and will look to us level
And straight as we near.

And the word will be *lawmaking*, made for us here as we stand
Not back home, not below, not down under,
But ready
And here at your hand.

* * *

Man himself
Taken aloof from his age and his country
And standing in the presence of Nature and of God
With his passions, his doubts, his rare prosperities,
And inconceivable wretchedness, is chief, if not sole,
Theme among these nations. Taken aloof.

*   *   *

Charles Neil, Kathy Caulfield, Kathy Csere,
Mary Lee Peyton, Gene Slear, and I, students all,
And Stephen Crane, George Stewart, James Dickey,
Ralph Ellison, Bill Corrington, De Toqueville, students all,
Have been riding around the Little Big Round Top the in the GTO,
Admiring the plenty of places to park.

But channel changes, windshield cracks, street feet
Get down to the ground
Walk over the plain ground,
To parley, in the presence of age and of country,
The chief and level theme
Of civil life.

FORTUNES

Chills were hopping in my skin
As I asked for a cup of tea
And my friend gave me also
A bag of fortune cookies.

Not one, not a handful, but a bagful.
That kind of bliss
Which steams from a cup of tea
Steamed to me.

Every probable, every possible,
Every impossible
Fortune from here to Mishima.
It was the world.

I cracked the first cookie, and it said
Do not open more than one
Of these fortunes
At a time.

CONCEPTION

Death did not come to my mother
Like an old friend.
She was a mother, and she must
Conceive him.

Up and down the bed she fought crying
Help me, but death
Was a slow child
Heavy. He

Waited. When he was born
We took and tired him, now he is ready
To do his good in the world.

He has my mother's features.
He can go among strangers
To save lives.

TOWARD I

When you turned away your attention
I turned mine away,
And I said, out of whatever corner of your interest
You have put me for safekeeping,
I will escape into peril.
And then the full bearing of your attention
In floodlight will veer upon me.
Oh, there you are.
And about time.

By some syllogism I still bring
Vengeance to myself that I see myself
Harried and at large down corridors
Of incapacity and perturbation where

Your presence, could it turn to me, would say,
Oh, there you are.
But the attention
Of your presence is diffused.

TOWARD II

Go out a little from yourself as you sit here,
Maybe to the path outside the window,
Maybe to an idea,
Or to in the next row an absorbing form.
Reject most of the lecture,
Most of your thought, most that the window bears,
Maybe the whole morning. There is being sifted
The sand of your time, turning as you turn.

I am beside you and we are exchanging
Several aspects of the ideas of history,
From their glosses there are being sifted
Sands of a time only becoming yours.
Sift me away and sift the whole morning.
Some day, not accountable, you may look down
To see in your palm as on a field of history
The grain of time you recognize as yours.

FAMILY

When you swim in the surf off Seal Rocks, and your family
Sits in the sand
Eating potato salad, and the undertow
Comes which takes you out away down
To loss of breath loss of play and the power of play
Holler, say
Help, help, help. Hello, they will say,
Come back here for some potato salad.

It is then that a seventeen-year-old cub
Cruising in a helicopter from Antigua,
A jackstraw expert speaking only Swedish
And remote from this area as a camel, says
Look down there, there is somebody drowning.

And it is you. You say, yes, yes,
And he throws you a line.
This is what is called the brotherhood of man.

AWAY

Never going off, always here, I
Never say goodbye. You may
Leave over and over, for good,
For the weekend, for my life; I
Wave and cry

What is my life but your leaving?
Giving a brief biography of my life, I say
Each year they are off, all of them,
Goodbye, goodbye,
Yet here I stay

As in 1940, 41, 58, 60, 70,
Now again they are going away.
Born yet unlearned in travel,
Each sacramental day
I give over
And they take it away.

from

Coming to Terms

1979

TRIP

We started from a station in the city,
Rough night, wind blowing rain slantwise
On the train windows.
Outside was the elegance of the station,
Hothouse roses in the areas
Of people saying goodbye,
Good luck.
We were the ones going
Into a tunnel of dark
Crying those going-away blues, going-away blues
In our long black woolen stockings and button shoes.
Hail, hail the gang's all here
Sang my father to the mahogany walls.
We were not listening and would not sing
What do we care. But we heard him.
The train pulled out of the station into Halloween,
The train pulled into November and the passengers between
Pumpkin and pumpkin gave us some good scares
To wile away the Halloween blues.
Three days and nights in the vestibules
Between cars, roaring and clashing at the heavy doors,
Closer to home than the outside scenes.
Then a little
Five-minute flash of home.
El Paso is The Pass, my mother said.
But it was rather
A burning deck of people in sombreros
Sitting against the sun. Rejoicing.
Now we could see orange trees, smell orange, that was a wonder,
And came through that garden to a narrow track
Of train on sand between mountains
Splitting against their ledges,
Nearly empty
The coaches, ledges, rocking along, seeking
Places to stop, with yellow stations
Under pepperwood, under water tank, under signal
Under sky
Nearly empty but our smoke blew in it.
All the baggage is gathered together, we stand
At the last vestibule, we are saying goodbye,
Good luck.

We pile down, look at the little
Boards of the station, turn away
Back to our black coaches, all of us in a row
In our black woolen stockings in the burning sun
To watch them leave us, pull away one by one
With a great grinding.
And they are gone.
And I see, what do we see, all of us,
Stretching my gasping eyes without air or kindness,
Sandy ranges of an infinite distance
Under a white-hot sky under
Infinite distance
Beyond a plain, a sea, a life of sand
Of infinite distance
No place to end. A breadth
Hurtful to any small heart,
A scope which beached our debris on its shore
Abandoned, lost from a tide of life.
Extended
Not toward us but away,
But we went to it.
Thirsty we drank its infinite sources,
Eyes brimmed with its tears.
A hotelkeeper in pith hat and jodhpurs
Drove our baggage into the Springs, in oasis,
But we had gone farther away.

BEFORE

Earlier, what I remember: a small
Flame of arthritis in the midst of fields
In the Euclidean Sunday mustard fields
And the mud fields of the potted palm,
In Jackie's airy room,
And at the fire station
All the brass
And all of us
Feeding the gulls.
A fresh salt breeze and foam
Around a plaster leg.

Away from the chloroform intern, joy
Of the long journey when I ran
Free of the plaster, and got back
Down those long hills, spent out.
Where had I been, oh tell me.
And where
Under those vast sunny
Apricot trees in the front yard?
Go tell Aunt Rhodie the old gray goose is dead.

BLOCKS

Earlier, many chloroformed halls went through,
White sheets lay on,
Masks breathed into,
Sotto voices calibrated.
They were all brick walls
Rising from root level below ground
To beyond eyesight
Standing across some sun.
Scotched by their presence,
Went with Mme. Montessori home again.

MOTIVE

A window in the shadowed room where I lay
Opened on a dark brick wall
And high beyond, the sooty block
Of buildings stood in rain.

Heat in bones under blankets burned
With aspirin. Keeping me warm,
What else? Grandfather shrugged.
Step-grandmother reheated the hot milk.

Later she brought also a small box
Which turned out to be filled with six small bottles
Of perfumes, assorted, six colors,
Oho! There is something to life!

DOLL

Though the willows bent down to shelter us where we played
House in the sandy acres, though our dolls,
Especially Lillian, weathered all the action,
I kept getting so much earlier home to rest
That medical consultation led to cast
From head to toe. It was a surprise for my parents
And so for me also, and I railed
Flat out in the back seat on the long trip home
In which three tires blew on our trusty Mitchell.
Home, in a slight roughhouse of my brothers,
It turned out Lillian had been knocked to the floor and broken
Across the face. Good, said my mother
In her John Deweyan constructive way,
Now you and Lillian can be mended together.
We made a special trip to the doll hospital
To pick her up. But, They can't fix her after all, my father said,
You'll just have to tend her with her broken cheek.
I was very willing. We opened the box, and she lay
In shards mixed among tissue paper. Only her eyes
Set loose on a metal stick so they would open
And close, opened and closed, and I grew seasick.

A friend of the family sent me a kewpie doll.
Later Miss Babcox the sitter,
After many repetitious card games,
Said, We must talk about bad things.
Let me tell you
Some of the bad things I have known in my life.
She did not ask me mine, I could not have told her.
Among the bad things in my life, she said,
Have been many good people, good but without troubles;
Her various stories tended
To end with transmigrations of one sort or another,
Dishonest riches to honest poverty; kings and queens
To indians over an adequate space of time.
Take this cat coming along here, she said,
A glossy black cat whom she fed her wages in salmon,
He is a wise one, about to become a person.
Come to think of it, possibly Lillian
Is about to become a cat.

She will have different eyes then, I said.
Obviously. Slanted, and what is more,
Able to see in the dark.

PARENT

Letting down the isinglass curtains
Between the wet rain and the back seat
Where new plaster flattened me, my father said,
Wait here. I will get you the sherbet
Of your eight-year-old dreams.
There were no drive-ins then.
The rain roared. Don't go away,
I said to him? He said to me.

ALBUM

This is a hard life you are living
While you are young,
My father said,
As I scratched my casted knees with a paper knife.
By laws of compensation
Your old age should be grand.

Not grand, but of a terrible
Compensation, to perceive
Past the energy of survival
In its sadness
The hard life of the young.

MARK

Irritated by the favoritism of Jehovah
Fatherhood of God,
I thought Cain
Into the wilderness. Southern Pacific
Set up in the mesquite trees
Yellow station boards

To split and wither in the shattering heat,
And there I saw
Necessity. Blessed necessity.
Blessed ground, blessed shade
Blessed telegraph, cactus
Necessity.
To which the vulnerable parent
Nodded and smiled.

VIOLETS

Flat markets in the flat rain,
Wet wool of being
Yet damper to receive in its sharpless squares
Hurtful if need be,
Whereas from my mother violets come to the wet wool,
From accidental deep bins of produce
And bespeak
Sources beyond price, beyond hesitation.

STUDY

At midnight dropping the beautiful
White net dress, I could not think
To be rid of it in sleep, to prepare
A flying spirit for a Saturday test.
There went joy, celebration, and there came
Heavy suppression to a lofty norm.

Saturday sulk and blur, eveyone went
To the beach, I to a Hall under vines.
The sun shone in, the topic was either,
To my reckoning, Progress of Science
Or Music in the Home. A sum of words.
There I prayed to friends, Franklyn, Frances, Dorothy, Roberta,
  as once to Welda,
Don't write on Murk in the Home! They did though.

My brothers were painting trim when I got to the cabin,
And said to our father, It is the wrong shade,

But my light heart jolted me out from that message,
To pause on the one I'd got in the afternoon light
Carved in the archway over that lively moss,
"Education is learning to use the tools
Which the race has found indispensable."

I thought, Good for Education, modest, and steadily
Learning its way. Out of that shabby gentle world of Melrose,
Out toward the sea and the ranges
Of Greek and geology. Learning the tools.

TEACHER

How did you come to be a teacher?
I went to work
In the Huntington Library in San Marino,
The many treasures unopened and uncut
Gave me pause.
Summer as it was, hot as it was, the best part of the day
Was a Chapman's ice cream cone with Jim Worthen,
Before Hollywood Bowl or Pasadena Playhouse,
To learn to write plays.
One practicing day in the heavy Fresno sunlight,
One practicing year in Berkeley fog,
Lehman, Caldwell, Lyon, Dennes,
The steady hearts of scholars made me be.

How did I come to be a teacher?
Another way.
On the street where I lived, two boys were going to college,
One to Cal Tech and one to Business School
—This is a little simpler than it was—
And both were in terrible struggles over learning
Especially by thought, like reason and consequence,
So I could help them.
That is pretty much of a joy
For fifteen to help nineteen and twenty-three
To engineer arguments, try Shakespeare, evaluate
Albers Mills for Dun and Bradstreet.
So that's how.

READERS

Jeff thinks
This is an angry text.
The professor asks how does he know.
Is he right? Will he profess?
Later today I will ask
Is it an angry text? Does he know my mind?
Over this famous text hovers a shadow.
Slowly it moves, the while in the temperate air
Flails Jeff's hand and flails mine,
I am angrier than he.
Sometimes with strength of resistance the teacher
Holds back the visible hands,
There is scarcely time for the lot,
And says listen and wait.
Protecting the text, protecting, then does he know
Jeff's anger and mine?

DISARMED

Here an establishment, its sunny rooms,
Noon offices and beings, vast competitive
Orders, clashes of temper,
Hope forward, elegant energy
Unfolded and disarmed me,
Turned to a love so swift it went
In and beyond that world like a free runner and found
Bodies of love out of belief.
Love of demeanor, love of that face and form
Just as it moved, seldom as I saw it
Put back together in my asking frame
A fortune of demeanor shapely and true.

SLACK

As slack mouth spills information,
Lip loosely widened slurs it,
Hand takes it on, curves and holds,

Wrist weighs, lays it along,
Gives it to me,
I accept, and thank the hand,
Though it's the slack says I'm welcome.

SLEEVE

This was a dark year for Spiro Agnew;
It was a dark year for me too.
I like fathers and brothers, I like to grow
Toward the height, following it, a shoulder of sun.

I lean on this shoulder and it bears me up;
Wide, well-suited, strong and square,
It holds my need, all I need
Rests there,

Substance of trust;
But this year touch my sleeve; my sleeve rends
In the dark, in the hidden dust,
To moth and rust.

FANATIC

Conference rolls on, chairs are hard,
Members on the flag-decked platform
Heard and unheard.

In the wings, doors watched by students,
Flutters of white, now and then, become
As out of vaults,

Multitudes of white-robed figures, arms lifted,
Flowing smoothly over auditorium seats
And consuming them.

Here and there little clusters of listeners
Sit tight. I sit tight and here
Phagocytes.

Clusters disappear, the silent fanatic
Coverage
Pure as fine linen.

BREAKFAST

Robert keeps in his parlor
A beautifully wrought casket
With a lady in it
Of Chinese descent, and a bouquet of orchids.

In his backyard he grows
Plots of chard,
And plucks it
Fresh as desire for dinner and breakfast.

Much comment
On the Swiss chard, its freshness, savor,
Sweetness, suitability, seems to prevent
Any comment on the orchid bouquet.

LUNCHEON

Jack Lyman came down from St. Helena for luncheon.
A warm day
In the vineyard valley, misty in Berkeley.
Rosalie Brown, *The Grasshopper's Man,* came, and Leonard Nathan,
Who Is Tolstoi, and Carol his wife.
Ask him
Were the eucalyptus groves in Berkeley like this then
When the Greek dancers danced in groves
As if fog, in chiffon? Where was the red wine
Inkiest in the city? How
Did Witter Bynner win those champions
From brief vignettes of song?

Later in the backyard
Leonard and I read the Rhymer's Club
To try to hear what they heard, but that wasn't it—
Those were ballads, in London, this may be George Sterling,
Evanescent?

At Arts and Crafts,
Kroeber, Cody's, Moe's, John's Soup Kitchen,
Far from the traffic of the Greek Theater,
They are crying or they are stammering
Creeley's halt lines.

So we ask Lyman at lunch,
As we would Hildegarde Flanner, Genevieve Taggard,
What did you hear then? Tell us how we can hear.
    Elusively, a sense of things unheard
    Awakes, and is forgotten as it dies.
    The afternoon is great with peace. Then cries
    Far off, and once, a bird.
From *Sails and Mirage and Other Poems,*
By George Sterling.

LUNCHEON 2

We met for luncheon to exchange views,
Soviet authors and ours, two Armenians
And a writer of children's stories,
Beef stew and jello, but no shared language,
So we say, Pasternak? No, no, their anger.
Gogol? More kindly, shake hands.
Sroyán? Aha! You happy people,
He walks among the pomegranate rows.

Dear friends, we exchange cards,
Minor titles and their authorship.
How much we know each other, drink our tea.
Then comes the tardy interpreter, checks all round
In Russian, and then asks us,
Why did you drop the bomb on Hiroshima?

NOON

Noon students slid onto the unfolded chairs
In the open square where Aldous Huxley stood.
He said, You will be told by those supposed
Wiser, that reason and intuition

Work together, support each other.
But that is false.
Reason is the great saboteur.
Do not believe otherwise.

Two o'clock class: What do I believe?
I believe otherwise.

GOODBYE

Did I make you angry? said Jim the Professor
To Daphne the four-year-old child.
She said nothing.

Please accept my regrets,
Said Jim the Professor
To Daphne. She said nothing.

I've got to go off to class now, said Jim
Astride his bike. Won't you say goodbye?
She said nothing.

Off down the road he went in a flurry of shirttails
Blurring into the wind, and rounding the corner
Out of sight. Goodbye, said Daphne.

OFFICERS

Mr. Hansen, the cop at the campus gate,
Put me through college.
While the dean of women
Advised against it, too complicated, the cop said,
You get enrolled some way, and I'll let you in.
Every morning, four years. On commencement day
I showed him my diploma.

Later when radio news announced Clark Kerr
President, my first rejoicing
Was with Mr. Taylor
At the campus gate. He shook hands
Joyfully, as I went in to a Marianne Moore reading.

And we exchanged over many years
Varying views of the weather.

Then on a dark night a giant officer came up to the car
When we were going to a senate meeting, strikebound by pickets,
And smashed his billy club down on the elbow of my student driver.
Where do you think you're going? I suddenly saw I knew him.
It's you, Mr. Graham, I mean it's us, going to the meeting. He
walked away,
Turning short and small, which he was, a compact man
Of great neatness.

Later when I taught in the basement corridor,
The fuzz came through,
Running, loosing tear-gas bombs in the corridor
To rise and choke in offices and classrooms,
Too late for escape. Their gas masks distorted their appearance
But they were Mr. O'Neill and Mr. Swenson.

Since then, I have not met an officer
That I can call by name.

MEMORIAL DAY

After noon, in the plaza, cries, shrill yells, running and breaking,
Students look desperately
Out of the open windows. We have to be there.
A rifle waves in the window,
Tear gas gusts in, no one to help
In the furtherance of this class in Milton's epics.
Well let's meet tomorrow at my house.
OK, we'll bring the wholegrain wheat-germ raisin bread.
Up in the office floors, out in the square,
Gas of a new kind in experimentation.
I choke and cry the tears they call for.
So I say, and now we are munching
Crunchies in the front yard,
And finishing the patristic part of Book VII,
Papers are due after the weekend,
Please go home and work there,
And tell your parents the story of these weeks.
Even if they believe in the war you're protesting,
They will believe you too. Tell them

The sorts of pressures, absences of aid,
Losses of understanding you are working under.
They say they've already tried: I get my dad on the phone
And he says You can't tell me.
Give me Mom, and my mom says
You can't tell me. Stay out of trouble.
The army helicopter
In its regular rounds of surveillance drops down low—
Our twenty figures in a courtyard may mean trouble.
Couldn't we pick these flowers to throw at them?
All these camellias overgrown and wasting?

INSTITUTIONS

At term end the institution slackens
And I have done poorly, not what I hoped.
So my thought is seized by other institutions
More terrible, where I would do less well.
Hospital, asylum, prison, prison camp,
And I fall into a reverie of dismay:
Failure to aid survival, failure to foster,
Failure to understand how the oppressions start.
End of term, cease of a striving heart.

Or term end and I have done well in it
Much that I hoped, much that I tried,
And I am caught from these visions into a stupor
Of all the more I have left untried.
Hospital, asylum, prison, tiger cage
Beyond my thought like a rift of cloud.
Shelter me from unending need, term end,
Begin a new demand.

FIGURE

A poem I keep forgetting to write
Is about the stars,
How I see them in their order
Even without the *chair* and *bear* and the *sisters*,
In their astronomic presence of great space,

And how beyond and behind my eyes they are moving,
Exploding to spirals under extremest pressure.
Having not mathematics, my head
Bursts with anguish of not understanding.

The poem I forget to write is bursting fragments
Of a tortured victim, far from me
In his galaxy of minds bent upon him,
In the oblivion of his headline status
Crumpled and exploding as incomparable
As a star, yet present in its light.
I forget to write.

BARRICADE

Work hard and fail,
Stop right at the wall,
Look around at the no-saying mouths, turn away,
What can you say? Walk away.

Pick up a new track, few there
Clear it away,
Press on in the clear air
And the breath
Of the others, and fail.

Stop in your track
At the sudden superfluous crowd saying stop,
Saying no. Pick up a trail
Dense as a jungle and friendly with friends, and go on
In a different direction
To rising and setting of sun
And be stopped, and say fail.

Shall you return?
By the barrows of age shall you move
Back on those tracks where the walls were?
Where are they now?
The bafflement comes to the resting and tiresome foot
Of a thousand of roads
All open, all asking traverse.

METAMORPHOSIS

At Johns Manville a miscalculation
Sent more asbestos fibers into the assembly-line air
Than would kill a cat. Tough Texans
Long laughed as they breathed.
After the first deaths, some investigations
By the Company, the Medical Profession, and the U.S. Bureau
    of Health
Came up with findings,
That is, with true facts,
That is with data, that is with knowledge.

And knowledge is power. The data
Were stacked on a high shelf and grew dusty
With asbestos dust.
Finally a young doctor, a student
Of mine, and I wish he were,
Got the stacks off the shelf.
Now the plant has been razed
And the coughers scattered to their various deaths.

Giant Texans breathing through calcium
Of too much recommended, it was said, milk,
Stir into the altitudes of the A.M.A.,
Of H.E.W. Johns Manville,
Some of your rough laughter, that they wake
You to their learning, making you put on
Their knowledge with their power.

BUREAU

Is this the University?
I'm calling about a letter of recommendation I want to withdraw.
What's the extension, 4101?
This is the Library.
Then how will I find the number of the Bureau
Of Employment, maybe it's Placement?
I'll give you the Director.
I merely want to withdraw and reword a letter.
This is Mr. McShaw, the Director. Yes, here is your item,
Professor, this is an excellent letter,

It must not be withdrawn.
Read Fowler, Strunk and White, any of the authorities,
You will see how well you have done here.
Pardon my exercise of authority,
But I cannot allow a good letter to be withdrawn.
Is this the University?
I am calling about bureaus, their hearts and minds.

BUREAU 2

Skunks fight under the house and keep us
Wakeful, they are down from the hills in the drought.
Lots of colloquial remedies, mothballs, tomato juice
Leave them unmoved. Call the S.P.C.A.
Call the Bureau of Health, call the P.G.&E. where they rest
Past the meter box, call the Animal Shelter,
Call commercial exterminators; all reply
With a sigh, and a different number to call
Next month or next year when they're not so busy.
Asking around, getting the number finally,
Number of the chief health officer of the county,
Mr. Simms. His secretary answers,
What makes you think Mr. Simms will speak to you?
What makes you think Mr. Simms is interested in skunks?
Mr. Simms is animal health officer of this whole county
And his chief interest is wolves.

MOVING IN

The telephone installer was interested
In the students helping me.
He said he had a father of 93, plus a mother 77,
And his wife kept running her heart out.
Students could help, what a good idea! Let me know
If at any time this telephone needs adjusting.

As he left, the upstairs apartment entered
With some slices of chocolate angel-food cake
To make herself acquainted.
She was a retired librarian and it turned out

The one librarian I knew in the town I came from
Was an old friend of hers, they both came
From South Dakota mining country.

The telephone installer returned to ask
If students were dependable? They can be.
Even more than a good chocolate cake, even more
Than a good telephone.
This could mean a new life for my wife and me, he said,
I think I'll bring you a longer cord for that phone.
Don't let this last piece of cake go begging, begged the upstairs apartment.

FUND-RAISING

When Genét came with the Panthers
To raise defense funds,
The Treuhafts stood him on a ladder before their old clinker-brick fireplace.
The bulky man,
Bursting in French English,
His clenched fist swayed the ladder, his wrath
Leaned into the social press.
He smiled at Masao, and spat also,
From his compact smooth density of resources.
Hilliard yelled, and others yelled
Until finally someone picked up a bottle
And threw it at someone.
It struck Michael McClure's young daughter
Where she sat on the hearth
And she sobbed, sobbed. Michael, schooled as a flame,
Leaped to the ladder and cried in a whisper
Victims! Always we have to have victims.
Down the steps of the porch, into cars,
Nobody there.

WHY WE ARE LATE

A red light is stuck
At the corner of LeConte and Euclid.

Numbers of people are going in and out of the 7 Palms Market,
Some sitting with beer at La Val's,
Lots lugging bags to the Laundromat—Open—
A couple thumbing rides up the hill, fog curling in over the
newsracks,
Low pressures.

You can tell it is about five or six o'clock
And we are coming home from a meeting not bad, not good,
Just coming along, and stop at the red light.
Time stands there, we in the midst of it,
The numberless years of our lives.
A late green light later
May let us get home.

EVENING NEWS

You know how the newsboy bikes through the stubblefield,
On the faint rough path between wild vines,
Into the condominium complex, the one hundreds
Then the two hundreds,
Hurling *Enterprises* as he rides?
Why does he suddenly ride in the opposite direction?
Why do the galaxies shift in the opposite direction?

AT THE COUNTER

Give me a half-sack of buttered popcorn, sweetie.
Would you like to hear some good news?
I'm a biochemist you know, even look like a biochemist they tell me,
Despite my rugged frame.
And today I discovered the cure for diabetes!
You may well exclaim.

You know what the cure is? An herb. It grows high
In the mountains of Mexico.
And my doctor tells me that my big chest cavity

Enlarged from singing opera will allow
My living as high as sixteen thousand feet
To cultivate the herb. What is its name?
I bet you'd like to know!

TRADE CENTER

When Leopold Senghor came to America
To negotiate with the President about imports
Such as lobster tails, he was asked at the White House luncheon
Whether he would go to Disneyland
As Khrushchev had not.
No, but, he said,
I will go to meet the boys of Hunter's Point
And the poets of San Francisco.
Seven o'clock, the wide windows of the Trade Center
Opened east over the bay,
To the low hills of Berkeley; lights and silver gleamed.
Senghor with his four short round ambassadors
Entered in French.
Where I sat listening in French, questioning in English
About alexandrines, the kindly interpreter
Wafted himself away from that metric region
Of half-understanding. At dinner
The Liberian ambassador, expert in American,
Put us into hilarity over the common procedures
Of Liberian diplomacy; would we not laugh we would cry,
How in his mint-julep stories we were children.
Then with a gasp
Poet and ambassadors pushed back their chairs,
Stood and bowed low
Out past the black windows to where in the east
Full over the hills into the blackest of summer skies, ascended
Their own moon.

PEARL

Inside the plane we went straight
Off the round earth into the round air,

Rounder, as if into a pearl,
A pearl's center, rounder, walls of pearl
Awash, luminous in the swim of pearl.

On our raft, luggage, small glasses, unexpandable
Into existences of milk and pearl,
Raft from Peoria, pitching in the sea
Of Galatea, floating
A few words of pidgin into pearl.

DELAY

Well, ladies and gentlemen, the tinned voice of the pilot said,
We seem to be having trouble with the landing gear,
Which is why you hear this loud shaking sound.
We are therefore returning to home port, hope to land
Without incident, will keep you informed.
The stewardesses worked on equipment in their booth.
Then many of the ladies and gentlemen
Moved from where they sat in holiday or business absorption
Over next to some child and engaged
In a great deal of peaceful conversation—
Reminiscences of their own, sighs, questions of the children,
Till the gear
Jolted itself into landing, and the pilot
Came on again, to regret the inconvenience.

TRAVELERS

The little girl was traveling unattached, as they say,
Closed into the window seat by a heavy
Businessman working on papers out of his briefcase.
From across the aisle another kept noticing
What help she needed, her travel case latched,
Her doll righted, coloring book straightened out,
And he kept leaning over across to assist her.
After a while the heavy-set man put away his papers,
Took out a small gameboard from his briefcase, and suggested,
How about a game of three-way parcheesi?

ISLAND

On the island each figure
Moves to become its island,
Down to the shore, enters
The surrounding sea.
Is surrounded
By the waves of its waters
Crowding its beaches.

A fringe of palms, or pines maybe,
Touches
Some outlying strand,
The center tingles
Toward opposite reaches.
Each figure
Wades fully into the waters of his island, saying
I am land.

LONE

Braking down a stretch of coast highway,
Enough sand shoulder for the VW to pull toward
When it starts dragging its rear end like a dog,
Back, how many miles of breakers?
Ahead, a promontory bend in the road.
No one passes, and the stillness extends.
Scrape the split axle around the point
And see what's there,
Some sort of joint beyond the marine zero?
Dragtail the pavement half-mile, mile, and turn
And there appear a leaning porch and pump,
Three signs: *Gas, Nehi, Wrecking Crew.*
They stand by the pump, the bottles in their hands.

INTENSIVES

Loving intensives of Intensive Care
Bear down on your given name,
Margaret, attend, attend now

Margaret, they call you to live intensely
At the moment of your medication.

What if for a while they call you Frances?
Enjoy this intensive
Error, it frees you,
You can float in Frances,
Sip Frances liquids.

What I wait for is the intensive moment
When you flip, turn over, look around.
Well hello, Dolly, back where
Hello, Dolly.
Where you belong.

SORROW

A tall stature of
Grave sorrow
Is what I embrace, its tenderness
Doesn't bend to me.
Straight

Sorrow descended
From cries in trees
Stands upright
Stiff at its waist
Where I reach,

Tells me but does not
Tell me.
Rather withholds
More than I can
More than man can.

WEED

As weed swells to its joint
      brittles its root
      slants at a bent

angle and
cracks in the sun, one
can believe
that many years have gone
since the green sprout sprang,
each flick of green
momentous as a time
to chew the remnant stem.

MANIFOLD

In the cabinet of analysis
Seeds group themselves by seed,
Catalogues invest a native cyclamen
Which knows no bond.

Curves to the manifold seem to subscribe
In parallel measure,
And in the flour bin the soy
Scatters to flour.

Lets off the hook a rigid
Marking of rights and signs
For the sake of savor,
Geometries of change.

BRIM

Less of time than the world allows
A repeated task, sinews not taking
Supposed messages, where will we be
Under the reign of senex? I absolve him
Of many miseries.

Curry another time, other worldly,
But here at home
Turn to skies in their wheeling
A simple crowded passage across the brim.

NADIRS

There were the clerks of the zenith and the figures,
There were winter-type clouds over the winter
There were summer-type clouds over the summer figures
And to speak to each there was a way, the same.
I went up to the clerk of the nadir and said See me
In noctions of one kind or another
Under a winter sun, and see safely to the zenith
How I welter under a blooming moon.
All is mine, but I like it
By each gesture toward the other or one.
So besit, said the clerks of the nadir
And the zenith as they turned to their own
Accounting of afternoon—
They were busy. How busy were they?
They required waiting in line
For the sun to go down over the eastern figures
And the moon to arise over the western figures
Moving from plane to plane.

EASTER

Cars drove in at angles
All around the flat adobe mission
Coming for mass.
White carnations
Were stuck before each saint of the desert
And tied with lavender ribbons.
A bucket held the water to be blessed;
A jug, the wine;
And the microphone kept tangling with tall candles
Before the lectern, before the altar.

Wiry twisted field workers came,
And polished uniforms from the air base;
And a group of sisters from the seminary
Made the responses sing in experienced voices,
Two hundred, because of the resurrection.
They had to push away the plywood back of the alter
And screen doors from the sides to take the numbers,
And the choir crowded in to make room.

Beside me sat three little dark girls
In yellow print dresses and crocheted stoles,
And before me their father, his heavy shoulders
Sloped over the slant of an easy hip,
His drawled notes to his wife with her beehive hairdo
Getting from her many worried frowns, sometimes a luminous
smile;
They followed their missalettes from page 26
To page 31, and page 56
And they brought him to the tomb.

Hello, folks, glad to have you with us
On this auspicious occasion when he is risen.
Some of you will want to take the blessed wine and the blessed
wafer
And receive communion. And this Evening mass will count
As a Sunday mass also. God be with you.
The tides that rose

In seas and trees
In the barometers of sealed test tubes
Rose with this moon over the desert
And I could see how the candles
Survived the entanglements of the microphones.
Everything there, in fact, rose from its tomb
And went along the road to Emmaus.

MAKERS

I would tell a tally of poets,
With their black interests
When they can eat, they pay.
Out of their nourishment they produce
Duck eggs, reindeer meat, seldom herbivorous.
Printers make their hearts go,
Run the links of their nucleic acids.
Small interest says our investor,
Small but compounded.

A letter out of the grain-filled San Joaquin Valley
Came to me whirlwind.
Change everything, be somebody else,
Commit other and less trivial sins,

That was my Brother Antoninus. But the great sins
Which the world at war called him to commit
He did not commit. He craved against his sainthood.

Change also said the telephone, crisp and direct.
Each of your syllables
Carries in its heart the flaw of corruption.
Reap them. Burn the wild grasses.
Rare, spare the honey, tender it
In equal conscience. I said I would not.
Now I must admire the orange trees
Of Howard Baker's Terra Bella, Winters'
Palo Alto airedales at their distance,
And hear meanwhile the bells of Martin's wife
True to the sharp edge which will incise
Truth; it cannot all be cut away.

In the hills behind, old Indian fighters,
Suffragettes, the vote scarcely won,
Readied to leave the vaulted blue-tiled well
Anytime for a New York jail.
They kept calling the journals all across the country
To wake up, get out a new edition
In pentameters if they couldn't manage a good *vers libre*.
And wake us still, dear Sara, Colonel, Caldwells,
Marie West, Taggard, Flanner into the chapparal
That will not slide the slopes but toughen
Into resolve to stick the firebreaks,
Sandy invasions and the hosts that blight the vines,
To draw the cup next year, new grapes.

Black to their coastal battlements
Sinclair Lewis wrote jokes for Jack London.
Somebody wasn't laughing. Jeffers bore
Human interest only at its darkest,
The resources of flesh against its stone,
Of time against its heritage, of lamb
Against its higher bird.

To the city it's a very slow commute, South San Francisco
And Daly City, delaying quite a while
By sense of a tolerable alternative,
Then that irascible Rexroth's Potrero. Change.
Or as a spark at the flint, Laurence Hart's
Give me an image of rain, just one

Brilliant notation of the brilliantly spitty rain.
Translator MacIntyre bruises so easy

Early like Ginsberg late prescribing
Dog piss in gardens. In his garden
Hidden away, its mint and lettuce
Not susceptible.

Diamant too, Gleason, Duncan, Spicer, Schevill, Elliott,
Ammons, Stafford,
To the city and away to change.
Now the many poets
Are hard on each other. When they have gone away
They will write, say
This is a terrible land. Change
The focus of affection, move to remake
Interest, move to remake
Capital, that they not destroy, that they
Preserve, to change.

Sometimes they move back, now they come
On motor bikes, wife and child and manuscript
In the hip pocket. Here they are! The three-year-old
Child up to the rostrum to recite.
Stores and cafes, churches and grammar schools
Take up the poets of peace and gladness, of dices and black bones,
Aisles laid back with easy riding.
Unaccountable
Now so many
Each in his own center
To let the new terms be negotiable,
The makers measure change.

CENTER

How did you come
How did I come here
Now it is ours, how did it come to be
In so many presences?
Some I know swept from the sea, wind and sea,
Took up the right wave in their fins and seal suits,
Rode up over the town to this shore
Shining and sleek

To be caught by a tide
As of music, or color, or shape in the heart of the sea.
Was it you?

Was it you who came out from the sea-floor as lab into lab
Weightless, each breath
Bubbling to surface, swaying in currents of kelp plants,
Came in your cars
Freewayed in valleys millions of miles from the shore
To converge where the highways converge saying *welcome to here,*
And to where?
To tape and percussion, raga computers,
Rare texts and components of clay,
With the sea down away past the freeways and out of the town
To the blockbusting towers of learning and quiet
Shades of administering redwood,
Azure dome over all like a bellflower
And star above star.

Did you come
Out of borderlands dear to the south
Speaking a language Riveran, Nerudan, and saying
Aqui estâ un hombre; my first lesson?
And come as Quixote, the man of romance
In its new century, tilting
At windmill giants of concrete,
Slim lance at the ready? Woe unto them
That join house to house, that lay field to field
Till there be no place that they may be alone
In the midst of the earth.
Did you come
With a handful of questions
Leaping like jewels
To shock answers, to start
Sparks of inquiry into the evening air?
I came as a kid
From that Midwest all recognize
As part of home,
To this another
Which the salt sea answered in its time
And Viscaino mapped his ports upon.
You came
As concertmaster of the Philharmonic
As mayor of Del Mar

As reader of magnetic messages in DNA
As archivist for the time's poetry, or PTA,
As land-grant scholar
Holding his gray moon rocks.

What is this that we come to,
Its walls and corridors
Gaping in space, its north lights
Seeking the north, its substance
Concrete brushed by the grains of its boards,
Its boards reaching extension in all of their lengths
In architectural solidity?
It is
A break in the galaxies of our imagination. It needs our lives
To make it live.

A building, a dark hole in space,
Compact of matter,
Draws into it buzzing disinterests,
Ideologies.
Incomplete being
Enters into the dense room, emerges
Another, further,
Compact of matter, this is the place that we enter,
It paints pictures here and plays drums.
It turns us around and we emerge
Out of old space into the universe.
This building
Between buildings as between galaxies,
Between fields as between flights of fancy,
Will reshape our ears and turn us,
Our work of art
Beating in the breast like a heart.

What are we here for?
To err,
To fail and attempt as terribly as possible, to try
Stunts of such magnitude they will lead
To disasters of such magnitude they will lead
To learnings of such magnitude they will lend
Back in enterprise to substance and grace.
What learning allows for is the making of error
Without fatality.
The wandering off, the aberration,
Distortion and deviation

By which to find again the steady center
And moving center.
What art allows for is the provisional
Enactments of such learning
In their forms
Of color and line, of mass and energy, of sound
And sense
Which bulk disaster large, create evil
To look it in its eye.
To forge
Villainies of the wars, to indispose
Villainies of petty establishment
To make them lead their lives in sound and sense
To no good end, that we may see them so.
To make mistakes
All of our own mistakes
Out of the huddle of possibilities
Into a color and form which will upbraid them
Beyond their being.

Give us to err
Grandly as possible in this complete
Complex of structure, risk a soul
Nobly in north light, in cello tone,
In action of drastic abandonment,
That we return to what we have abandoned
And make it whole.
Domesticate the brushed
Cement and wood marquee,
Fracture the corridors,
Soften the lights of observation and renew
Structural kindness into its gentler shapes.

Out of the sea
The kelp tangles, out of the south
The cities crowd, out of the sky
The galaxies emerge in isolation
One from another, and the faces here
Look one to another in surprise
At what has been made.
Look at the actual
Cliffs and canyons of this place,
People and programs, mass and energy
Of fact,

Look at the possible
Irradiating all these possibilities.

Praise then
The arts of law and science as of life
The arts of sound and substance as of faith
Which claim us here
To take, as a building, as a fiction, takes us,
Into another frame of space
Where we can ponder, celebrate, and reshape
Not only what we are, where we are from,
But what in the risk and moment of our day
We may become.

Recent Uncollected Poems

1960s-80s

VIGILS

We are talking about metaphor.
The fog comes in as Sandburg says it does,
Dark over our streetlights and our houses.
What Jim says of metaphor Fred cannot abide
And I cannot abide, but in more silence.
Look, we are getting nowhere, it is midnight,
Get home out of this warm firelight into the fog,
We will solve them yet, metaphors,
Their common properties.

Later from their lab the physicists
Come for their friends and hear a poem or two.
How they hear the wrong ones, the right go by them,
And folks go off to buy the daily bread, pale,
Not yet reinforced with wheat germ.
How do we survive? Do we survive?
The red shift startles us, the solid state,
That dialectic,
And such wonders as would drive us out
Into the attics of our driven friends,
Vigils of the academic dark.

POISE

His dad holds his hand; his suspenders,
His pants. Vital as is that hand in hand, that rubberized
Elastic, powerful as the Nietzschean life force, frees
His steps into the stride of such poise, of such assured proportion
A humanist would recognize the kind.

VOTE

Be sure, said my mother, holding my hand
As we spoke to the ladies, door after opened door
In the sunny neighborhood, Be sure
Once we've the vote, war will cease,
We will go to the polls, we will speak our piece,

And there will be no more war.
Then I was four.
Still the ladies in the sunny neighbor air
Register faithfully, do they not, their care
For no more war?

RECOGNITION

Known before, painfully learned before,
Conceived before and cogitated,
Tested and proved, hated and loved before
And abated.

Known again, painfully known again,
Made and remade,
As if for the first time, the first word
First said.

AIM

Every year when I come to hate
I am ashamed of it,
A very fever fit
Which must at last abate.

This year alone I have
Only the fit of love
And in its radiance
Look down look down on shame.

But then beneath I am
Holding for very life
To all that hateful strife
That gives to love its aim.

SLEEP

What sleep obliterates, it manufactures.
It has taken a gangling look over the world,

Told old stories or reversed them.
What of the night? It is noon rather,

Or it is Gandhi, what he tells
Is intriguing. Don't interpret
How meaningful is life, but how halfway
It will wake you up.

PROMISE

He said: I do not lie; the institution
Of which I am a pillar may lie
Because it has no memory.
It cannot promise
Because it cannot remember, so it sweetly
Avers, and that is an end to it.
One may change his life for it, but the place not notice.

He said, Once I signed a contract and the place
Signed a contract in its own blood
Which was the flow of paper. From it was erased
Daily its promises, so it would remember
Nothing uneasy. I was uneasy,
Alive on that slope of contract
Slipping into the circula file by nightfall.

He said, What if I would learn to tell a new lie, like All is chaos,
And then build out of that rubble a satisfaction
Of promises, saying
So it was in the days of my arrival
And so today. Against the river of Heraclitus
Stand the possible pillars
Of those who would aver into the future,
For whom the future is verifiable
In words even on paper in the means of life.

FACES

Withheld, cruel even, and even besotted,
Their faces allowed to be seen
One to one, their miseries ballooning

Into the dreams of the populations,
No one excepted.
Everyone facing in darkness one of those monsters,
Cruel even, custodial, jailer and master,
The millions of history put to this shame.

How does it happen that some
Grow up among faces not cruel not destroying
But fresh as the day,
Seeing not us but themselves, looking one way
Eyes open, smiles ready,
The radiance of learning upon them,
The portable treasure of dream?

IONS

There comes this day
Never expected, a first day
In air, lungs breathing
Air from somewhere else.
Warm to touch,

Irritable rustles in it like news from other states
Come as if to arrive on this day today.
Some leaves leave their trees,
Now I will realize
Which go, which stay.

SUBJECT

Tell me about happiness
  It is the air
    Breathes in and out
    Bothers the heart
    Opens trees
    Quiets the thunder, or reflects it,
  Sits there beaming.
Is it you? Happiness?
  Hold out a string of words
  That I may see

Before you come to be, how you will take
Every letter and space into your hand
To your absolving hand.

AFTERNOON WALK

There is this old man, wistful, peaked,
Going to mail his letters,
Formerly a governor of some renown.
Good morning, I see you are going to mail your letters.
Yes, I am going to mail my letters.

This peaked old man suddenly
Looks out of the profiles out of the eyes of friends
Smiling, what a strained happening.
Mortality, are you going to mail your letters?
Yes, I am going to mail your letters.

HOME MOVIES

Quick, into the house, bring out the baby,
Rosettes in her hair. Sparkle, baby!
See now she dances with her baby brother,
Pushes his carriage nearly off the steps.
To the rescue! Five or six neighbor children
Get into the picture too, and there's their mama,
Her husband is now head of R, P, and M;

See her short hair-do?
There we are all fishing
Up on the Klamath. Jerry is clowning as usual
Doing the Charleston. Oh, the babies have fallen
Into the mud, aren't they a sight, we're jumping
Just to keep warm, maybe mosquitoes,
Maybe the speed of the film.

What are they called, these charges,
Volt upon volt, ion and ion of energy
Sparked from the film and racing.
Picking the kids up, dusting them off, taking their pictures,

Fred's too, he's so handsome; year after year
The Mack Sennett motion, chase of the comic?
To live, and to live.

CAGE

Through the branches of the Japanese cherry
Blooming like a cloud which will rain
A rain white as the sun
The living room across the roadway
Cuts its square of light
And in it fight
Two figures hot, irate,
Stuck between sink and sofa in that golden cage.

Come out into the night, walk in the night,
It is for you, not me.
The cherry flowers will rain their rain as white
Cool as the moon.
Listen how they surround.
You swing among them in your cage of light.
Come out into the night.

STREET

In the house you live in
The television
Burns blue in the family room,
The kitchen in white and yellow tile sparkles
By its refrigerator, and the headboards
Bear lights for a long reading of *Time.*
Where do the children do their homework now,
At the dining table, at their desks
Painted by you? And when the dog runs
Where does he run to between your house and the next?
Is it a runway, is it lawn or hedge?
If I am driving down your street in the evening
Looking for a number, your house can be mine
As well as the next.

ENCHANT

When I went to a friend's funeral
An encantment had changed the people there,
Bent their backs, flattened their shoes off
Untied their heads,

And I saw I needed an enchantment
To be transformed also, so I might bend
Into the perilous shape not of my vague spirit
But of a friend.

STROKE

I should like to hurry to get back into the world.
I am so far from it, eyes, ears blurred,
Memory forsaken.
Rumors of what's going on
I would urge to be longer, stronger.

What did you say? I say
The voices I hear
Ring out from a round bell from far away,
Hurry up! What is your hurry?
Strike me back into the world.

SUBDIVISION

Tiled fences run a mile along the freeway,
Roofs sliding snow,
But walls with porthole windows set for sea.
Who has lived here? Family upon family
Running to school, meeting the evening news
As in the milky way,
Commuter lawn in jeans in play to play.
Who lives here now?
It is the Arabs.

Veiled, they stare from the veiled multitude
Of venetian blinds,
Hold over their noses their polyster shawls.
Inside kids keep cable going.
Gradually in the quiet street will the cries
Of games again arise?
What games?

WEST FROM ITHACA

When we went out to a country inn for dinner,
We turned west at crossroads, west
Between maples, west
Toward a straight ridge of hills, where the sun was setting.
There's your west, Walter said; Berkeley.

But I saw the long labs and markets
In Illinois, of afternoons not yet ending,
High plains, Boulder, the descent
To Salt Lake, cattle and presses driving in Boise,
And somebody practicing sailing on the Bay.

Now it was dark, there was manifest Tsingdao,
Though I could go no farther now it was dark.
What do you really see in that streak of light over the ridge?
I asked Walter.
Your west, he said.

CAPITOL

Status jonquils, to green to red lights, at successive circles
At Capitol Hill:
How can I call out and be answered?
A telegram will fly so fast through the corridors
A note so slow it hangs mid-air Smithsonian
Among the old wheels.

What can be heard in the pavane

To catch a wavelength from Loudon County,
From Texas fields, eastern shores
Where they are pacing, where they are dancing
The dance of traffic, its monoxide flow,
Its architectural design
Receding and ceding, in the magnificent spheres
Of influence?

WORLD

Coming up against the end of the world,
I saw how frayed it was,
Sleazy, ill-conceived,
What an ending,
Trumped up, frazzled like our fears,
And I wondered why. On what island
Or delta or forest of aloes
Could we settle the seams of our determination?

Now I must turn to look around to see
In my own shadow
Retrieving, unretrieving
Could we find menders, could we take up the thread
Of all this ravel,
To piece together a pattern for the world?

FOR MAGISTRATES

Mirrors for magistrates, for them a time
Beyond them, yet themselves.
Retrace into their faces
Fortunes of their fall, and how they see
How now they judge, the witnessing they do
Ready for life again.
Beyond the Percys and the peanut farmers, a judge,
Sirica's migrant youth, capacious age.
Lenses left
Now by so much refraction,
And platelets in the blood will correspond

To platelets in the basics of the sea,
Lifting and falling, till the satellite
Mirrors reflect a life in consequence.
And justice learns again its portraiture.

* * *

To the bar of justice comes Owen Glendower
Starved from Wales, the mountains of the north.
Is it fate or fault says Owen Glendower
That brings me to this mirror of my life?
I will say to you William Baldwin, judge and listener,
And your associates here, Believe me
I pray you Baldwin since you do intend
To show the fall of such a chief too high
Remember me, whose miserable end
May teach a man his vicious life to fly.
Such idle youth as wait upon the spoil
From every part of Wales unto me drew,
For loitering youth untaught in any toil
Ready all kinds of mischief to ensue.
Her shame and pain a while were at a strife,
Pain prayed me yield, shame bade me rather fast:
The one bade spare, the other spend my life,
But shame (shame have it) overcame at last.
Whereby (O Baldwin) warn all men to bear
Their youth such love, to bring them up in skill
And not presume to climb above their states,
For they be faults that foil men, not their fates.

* * *

Says Howard Hunt, humbly,
Humbly with profound contrition I request
Your honor to look beyond the Howard Hunt of June
To my life as a whole, and if it please the court,
Temper justice with mercy.
My fate and that of my family and children
Is in your hands.

His fate was in his own
Hands says Judge Charles Sirica. This book in 1559
Of William Baldwin's
Can show as in a mirror to move you
To the soonest amendment; Henry Percy,
Richard, Duchess of Gloucester, Buckingham,

Their coming to us here to tell their stories.
Most young people will see that our system
Works as our founding fathers hoped it would,
And that it must be nurtured and preserved.
That January morning in 1973
The ceremonial courtroom on the sixth floor was crowded.
From the massive gray marble hall
Hammurabi, Justinian, and Solon
Stared over my shoulder reminding me
Of the tradition of law I hoped to be upheld.

* * *

How many honey locusts have fallen,
Pitched root-long into the open graves of strip mines,
Since the First World War ended
And Wilson the gaunt deacon jogged sullenly
Into silence? James Wright remembers:
America goes on, goes on
Laughing, and Harding was a fool.
Even his big pretentious stone
Lays him bare to ridicule.
I know it. But don't look at me.
By God, I didn't start this mess.
Whatever moon and rain may be,
The hearts of men are merciless.

* * *

Some city councilmen here believe
The franchise question is the most important in their
  tenure,
The desires of their constituents, the demands
Of interest groups. In the worst instance
The result may be lying, cheating, finally bribery.
Gustave M. Hauser, president and co-chairman
Of Warner Amex, in active pursuit of franchise
Says, there is discretion in those decisions
And where there is discretion there is politics.
Magistrate Riley, what is your decision
While my little one, while my pretty one, sleeps?

* * *

Tragedy of a peasant emperor,
Ruler of a quarter of mankind,

Basking in the applause of foreign scholars,
Led to confusion, doubt, disaster,
Pride held him and he could not tell his story
To Baldwin. He forced
Stories from others till the mirrors clanged
Cracked in the harvest of a hundred flowers.
Jiang Qing
Cracked in the regime.

*   *   *

The questions are obvious but the answers aren't
  simple.
Sirica says he had no idea how hard it all would be,
How complex were the barriers being thrown up
To keep the court in the dark.
Who could have guessed how high this case would reach,
That the most powerful men in American government
Would begin a desperate struggle to save their own
  careers?
Humbly and with profound contrition I request—
The precepts of fair trial and judicial objectivity
Do not require a judge to be inert.
A combination of accident, luck, Providence
Has controlled my life.
The distance from a poor and struggling family
To the federal bench
And to a confrontation with the most powerful man in
  the world
Is nearly incomprehensible. His fate,
Sirica says, is in his own hands.

*   *   *

Shaving, an uncle asks,
What is this face before me in the mirror?
Look well, children, for you see
A face that may grow handsomer every day.
Not Alger, not Narcissus in the steam.

*   *   *

Gazing at it, would the martyr ghost
Returned from the grave
Ask, Is this the face I shaved?
As we search the photographs, bearded to full-whiskered,

We watch a man not yet forty
Who might be years younger
Develop into an ageless ancient, which indeed his secretaries
called him.
He would be considered no worldly success till late in his
career
But his many failures read
Less as mischance than as apprenticeship.
The superiority of Abraham Lincoln over other statesmen
Lies in the limitless dimension of a conscious self,
Its capacities and conditions of deployment.
In 1863 Walt Whitman watched him
During some of the worst weeks of the war.
I think well of the President. He has a face
Like a Hoosier Michael Angelo, so awfully ugly
It becomes beautiful, with its strange mouth,
Its deep-cut crisscross lines,
And its doughnut complexion.
Suffering endured stoked his energy
With penetration and foresight, often hidden from contemporaries,
Visible
Through restored photos.

* * *

Hear Arguedas saying,
Don't run away from me, come close!
Take a good look at me, recognize me.
How long must I wait for you?

Come close to me; lift me to the cabin of your helicopter. I will toast you with a drink of a thousand different flowers, the life of a thousand crops I grew in centuries, from the foot of the snows to the forests of the wild bears.

I will cure your weariness, which clouds you; I will divert you with the light of a hundred *quinua* flowers, with the sight of their dance as the winds blow; with the slight heart of the lark which mirrors the whole world;

I will refresh you with the singing water which I draw out of the black canyon's walls. . . .

Did I work for centuries of months and years in order that
someone I do not know and does not know me
cut off my head with a small blade?

* * *

Sam Kagel's *Anatomy of an Arbitration:*

UNION: Would you give your full name to the reporter, please?
GREEN: Mrs. Ann Green.
UNION: What is your occupation, Mrs. Green?
GREEN: I'm a grocery clerk.
UNION: How long have you been a grocery clerk?
GREEN: Oh, about ten years, I guess.
UNION: What was your last employment?
GREEN: I worked for the Z Grocery Store. I was a checker there.
UNION: For how long?
GREEN: I guess about four years.
UNION: Have you ever been discharged from any employment?
GREEN: You mean in the grocery business?
UNION: Yes.
GREEN: No.
UNION: Now, would you describe in your own words how you happened to leave your employment at the Z Grocery Store?
GREEN: Well, on this day—I've forgotten the date—I think it was referred to here already—I was doing my usual duties, and Red over there, the manager, came to me and he says, "Go wash those front windows." I had washed them before but every time I washed them I'd tell him I didn't think I should do it, that wasn't my work, that was the janitor's work. But he kept telling me I should wash them. I kept protesting. And then he just ordered me to do it and I told him then I didn't think I had to do it because the union agreement didn't say I had to do it and he told me—and he used pretty threatening language I thought, the way he said it— in effect, he said, "You better do it." So I washed the windows.

* * *

I have heard of the Warren Court and the Burger Court
And the indeed small claims court, where sometimes
Justice is done, and the world court. Lawless resolutes
Clanning from Wales and urban Africa
Come to be king and come then to the bar
Where suffering reigns, providence has its play,
The mirrored bar where Hammurabi dwells,
And Solon says the heart is merciless.
But renders justice, that it will survive.

INDEX OF FIRST LINES

A NOTE ON THE AUTHOR

JOSEPHINE MILES, a native of Chicago, is University Professor of English, emerita, at the University of California at Berkeley. Her ten volumes of poetry include *Coming to Terms, To All Appearances, Fields of Learning, Kinds of Affection, Civil Poems, Neighbors and Constellations, Prefabrications, Local Measures, Poems on Several Occasions,* and *Lines at Intersection*. Widely recognized as a scholar, Miles has also written numerous volumes of criticism including *The Vocabulary of Poetry, Eras and Modes in English Poetry, Style and Proportion,* and *Poetry and Change* (Lowell Prize winner).

POETRY FROM ILLINOIS

History Is Your Own Heartbeat
Michael S. Harper (1971)

The Foreclosure
Richard Emil Braun (1972)

The Scrawny Sonnets and Other Narratives
Robert Bagg (1973)

The Creation Frame
Phyllis Thompson (1973)

To All Appearances: Poems New and Selected
Josephine Miles (1974)

Nightmare Begins Responsibility
Michael S. Harper (1975)

The Black Hawk Songs
Michael Borich (1975)

The Wichita Poems
Michael Van Walleghen (1975)

Cumberland Station
Dave Smith (1977)

Tracking
Virginia R. Terris (1977)

Poems of the Two Worlds
Frederick Morgan (1977)

Images of Kin: New and Selected Poems
Michael S. Harper (1977)

On Earth as It Is
Dan Masterson (1978)

Riversongs
Michael Anania (1978)

Goshawk, Antelope
Dave Smith (1979)

Death Mother and Other Poems
Frederick Morgan (1979)

Local Men
James Whitehead (1979)

Coming to Terms
Josephine Miles (1979)

Searching the Drowned Man
Sydney Lea (1980)

With Akhmatova at the Black Gates
Stephen Berg (1981)

More Trouble with the Obvious
Michael Van Walleghen (1981)

Dream Flights
Dave Smith (1981)

The American Book of the Dead
Jim Barnes (1982)

Northbook
Frederick Morgan (1982)

The Floating Candles
Sydney Lea (1982)

Collected Poems
Josephine Miles (1983)